Why God Why?

Sermons on the Problem of Pain

Justin W. Tull

PROTESTANT PULPIT EXCHANGE ®

Abingdon Press
Nashville

WHY, GOD, WHY? SERMONS ON THE PROBLEM OF PAIN

This book is printed on recycled, acid-free paper.

Library of Congress Cataloging-in-Publication Data

Tull, Justin W., 1945-
    Why, God, why? : sermons on the problem of pain / Justin W. Tull.
        p.   cm. — (Protestant pulpit exchange)
    Includes bibliographical references (p.   ).
    ISBN 0-687-00702-X (pbk. : alk. paper)
    1. Suffering—Religious aspect—Christianity—Sermons.   2. Pain—
Religious aspects—Christianity—Sermons.   3. Sermons, American.
I. Title.   II. Series.
BT732.7.T85   1996
248.8'6—dc20   95-41093
                                                                                        CIP

Scripture quotations, unless otherwise indicated, are from the New Revised Standard Version Bible, Copyright 1989 by the Division of Christian Education of the
National Council of the Churches of Christ in the USA. Used by permission.

Scripture quotations noted RSV are from the Revised Standard Version of the
Bible, copyright 1946, 1952, 1971, by the Division of Christian Education of the
National Council of the Churches of Christ in the USA. Used by permission.

The poem on page 102 is from *Christmas Is for Celebrating,* by Melvin E. Wheatley,
Jr., © 1977 by the Upper Room. Used by permission.

The Advent devotion on pages 100-101 is from *Advent, A Calendar of Devotions,* by
Margaret Anne Huffman, © 1992 by Abingdon Press. Used by permission.

97 98 99 00 01 02 03 04 05 — 10 9 8 7 6 5 4 3 2

MANUFACTURED IN THE UNITED STATES OF AMERICA

"Friends and family? Where are they in my need?" some would say. But in health and in pain, my loved ones have been there for me, showing love and concern and positive words. From so many places, for so many years, I have been remembered by loving family and loyal friends. "I've had it all."

Some say they never had the time to volunteer and give their time to helping others through church and in community. They say, "Don't take me now, Lord. I just now have the time to give to others." I asked my community to let me serve their children and they said "yes" and elected me. After six years they said I was a good citizen. I felt so honored. "I've had it all."

For fifty years I have lived my life with few regrets. I have lived with love surrounding me and wonderful opportunities abounding. I cannot shake my fist and rail at any injustices dealt me, because it seems to me, "I have had it all," (Spring, 1994).

Loretta Pond, to whom this book is dedicated,
battled courageously with cancer for seven years.
As a close personal friend, it was difficult to accept the news of the onset
of her illness at the early age of forty-three. Her lengthy battle ended on
January 18, 1995.
During her illness, which was often filled with pain and debilitating
weakness, I know that the question "why?" was raised by Loretta, her
family, church members, and friends. But her final wrestling with this
basic human question did not end in bitterness, resignation, or despair.
Some prose, "I've Had It All," that she wrote less than a year before her
death reflects her ultimate stance of gratitude.

I've Had It All

by Loretta Pond

Some people rail at death. There wasn't time to gather memories of the world and all its mysteries. They yearn for life's experiences, to travel to China and Hong Kong, Singapore and Italy, Germany and exotic tropical islands. And I reply, "I've done it all."

Some would say that love has cheated them. "I'll die alone," they cry. But I could never say it. I had one man to love me and he was always there—my rock in times of fear and suffering, a faithful partner, my best friend. "I've had it all."

Some cry that they cannot leave their children. In spite of age they have much growing up to do. They make wrong choices, are indifferent to responsibility, and their efforts are lazy. My children are beautiful in their hearts and in their ways. They take responsibility for learning what was taught, their values are high. I do not leave them knowing there is more they need of me. How blessed I am. "I've had it all."

Contents

Introduction

One of the most important roles of preaching is to be a catalyst for theologizing. The preacher is to assist the individual church member in formulating a theology that is consistent with the gospel while being able to withstand the tough tests of life. It is not acceptable to preach positive platitudes or offer trite answers to life's profound tragedies. It is not acceptable to escape existential questions with a simple pastoral instruction to embrace everything on faith or to promote the false notion that somehow every tragedy is God's will.

Throughout my ministry, I have endeavored to deal honestly with questions of human suffering and pain. I have sought the biblical witness as it has addressed such human dilemmas. This series of sermons evolved primarily out of the crucible of life experiences. They all have in common the human cry of "why?" "Why all this suffering? Why the injustice? Why does God allow evil to exist? Why did this tragedy occur?"

Sermons that focus on these questions may be spawned

by national tragedies like the burning of the Davidic compound near Waco or the bombing of the federal building in Oklahoma City. Events such as these cry out for a word from our pulpits. At these times of human tragedy people everywhere ask, "Why, God, why?"

But sermons that ask, "Why, God, why?" may also come out of pastoral care. A parishioner who is critically ill may raise a theological question to her pastor: "What did I do to deserve this?" A congregation deserves to know how its minister will answer such a question—not from a bedside, but from the pulpit, drawing upon the biblical witness.

One of the sermons of this book came after a series of deaths within the congregation just prior to Christmas. It did not seem appropriate that I preach simply a positive word of "joy to the world" without acknowledging in some way that there was also sadness within our own congregation. I decided to preach using the text from Matt. 2:16-18 that introduces the tragic deaths of innocent children at the hand of King Herod at the very time of the coming of the Christ Child. By drawing from the text and the Christmas story, I sought to find a word of hope and joy even for those overcome with sorrow.

At other times these existential sermons have evolved not from the human condition but from the text itself. There are texts that raise their own theological issues as in the case of John 9:1-2: Is blindness caused by sin?

In preaching, one can search for the biblical witness that addresses a prevalent theological issue raised within the congregation. One may also share the theological insight of a biblical text that indeed intersects with the theological wrestling of the present day. Either way, it is the responsibility of the preacher to address the tough theological questions of the person in the pew. One of the most prevalent questions throughout human history is the question, "Why, God, why?" These sermons attempt to address this most basic of all human questions.

> *Rejoice in the Lord always; again I will say, Rejoice. Do not worry about anything, but in everything by prayer and supplication with thanksgiving let your requests be made known to God. Philippians 4:4-6*

Why, God, Why?

*H*ave you ever asked the question, "Why, God, why?" Have you ever asked, "Why did this have to happen to me?" or "Why did God allow this to happen to my friend?" Have you ever wondered if people really deserve all the bad things that come their way? If you have asked one or all of these questions, you join millions who when faced with tragic circumstances raise their cries of agony, or confusion, or protest.

> *Have you ever asked, "Why did this have to happen to me?"*

When was the last time you asked, "Why, God, why?" Was it because of a death, an illness, a hardship, a tragedy, an injustice, or an inconvenience? Or maybe when bad things happen that affect your life you don't formally challenge God; maybe you just become angry, absorbed in self-pity or cynicism. But your underlying question—sometimes even unspoken—is this: "Why did this have to happen? Surely this is not God's plan or will . . . so why didn't God do something to prevent it?"

Many of us do ask this basic question as we face troubling

9

circumstances. We may ask it when a child is seriously ill and suffering. We may ask why when someone suffers a betrayal. We may ask this most agonizing question when an innocent youth is shot and killed or when a young child dies. We may ask why when our life's savings are wiped out, when we lose our job, or when the spouse we have loved for so long dies.

We may even ask why when simple inconveniences come our way. Do you feel a bit mistreated when your air conditioner dies a premature death or when your car is in the shop more often than you attend church? Do you ever wonder if you are jinxed, if you are preordained to bad luck? Do you sometimes get the feeling that life is designed to test your patience and courage?

Sometimes it is not *one* tragedy that forces us to raise our question of doubt and protest. Sometimes it is the sum total of many, many things that add up to one big question mark. Maybe after experiencing many setbacks in a row we conclude that life just hasn't been that good to us.

One of the challenges of our existence is that we never really know what is in our future. If we count on job security, we may find ourselves laid off or disabled. If we dream of a relaxed and secure retirement, we may discover dwindling funds, or have to assume guardianship of a grandchild, or find ourselves working again just to get by.

Most of us, even the luckiest among us, have asked this question many times—if not for us, then on behalf of some good person who suffers. We lift our appeal or our protest, "Why, God, why?" "Why did this have to happen?" "Why should this happen to her?" "Why did this come along? Everything was going so well!"

Some religious people insist that we have no right to question God or to raise our voices in protest. They contend that God is in control of everything and that God knows what to do in all circumstances. They tell us that no matter how tragic it seems to us, it is all a part of God's plan.

I do not embrace such a theology, and neither would the psalmists. I believe that God cries with us when tragedy comes. I believe that it is not a part of God's plan for an assassin's bullet to strike down a president or a civil-rights leader, or for stray bullets to kill innocent bystanders. It is not meant to be!

> *When tragedy strikes, God suffers with us.*

I don't believe that every car I have bought that has proved to be a "lemon" was produced that way to teach me patience. At least, if that was the plan, it has not worked! Instead, I believe that God empathizes with all our trials and tribulations. When tragedy strikes, God suffers with us. Maybe in the midst of tragedy we should delay asking *our* question and first hear God's prior question: "Indeed, humanity, why *did* this happen?"

But as important as this basic question is, in the midst of hardship, suffering, or tragedy, there is another issue worth exploring. In a sense it is the same question, but the perspective is inverted, the tone is different, the motivation is reversed. Surprisingly, the question becomes not one of protest, but of praise; not one of bewilderment, but of wonder; not one of cynicism, but of promise.

I purposely began my reflections where probably 90 percent of us start when we ask, "Why, God, why?" I started with the bad things. And isn't that what comes to mind when you hear the question "Why, God why?" If you read the title "Why, God, Why?" before reading the sermon, did you expect me to focus on blessings or hardships, windfalls or downfalls, sickness or good health? I suspect most of you gravitated toward the negative.

My assumption is this: most of us ask, "Why, God, why?"

in the midst of misfortune. But when good things come our way we rarely ask, "Why did this have to happen to me?" When we experience good fortune we rarely protest: "I just don't deserve this!" When life smiles upon us we seldom ask, "Why, God, why?" We rarely ask, "Why me, Lord?"

> *When we experience good fortune we rarely protest: "I just don't deserve this!"*

I remember clearly when this thought first occurred to me. It came to me in the early seventies when I was riding my bike to make a pastoral call at a nursing home. The thought suddenly dawned on me, "Why do we ask, 'Why, God, why?' when bad things happen but seldom ask that same question when good fortune comes?" It then occurred to me that maybe our problem is not in asking, "Why, God, why?" too often. Maybe we ask the question too seldom!

> *Our problem is not in asking, "Why, God, why?" too often. Maybe we ask the question too seldom!*

Before preaching this sermon I shared my novel thesis with another minister. He seemed unusually intrigued with what I assumed was an original insight. But, alas, the next day he handed me a sheet of paper with several quotes. One was circled. To my shock there was my "unique" idea in print.

Seeing it there sparked two simultaneous but diverse feelings. It made me feel good that someone else had come to the same conclusion. I was flattered that my idea was already in print even though it was attributed to another person. But my ego was also somewhat deflated because my insight must have been more obvious than I first imagined. Listen to this quote from Irene Bargmann of Columbus, Nebraska: "When sorrow comes, we have no right to ask, 'Why did this happen to me?' unless we ask the same question whenever joy comes our way."[1] So there you have it, practically my whole sermon in twenty-six words!

I would therefore suggest that we never forbid asking the question, "Why, God, why?" I would urge instead that we boldly expand its application. We should apply it generously to life and to the Scriptures.

So now we ask not simply, "Why did the prodigal son leave his father and waste his inheritance?" We ask the question of grace: "Why, God, did the father find it in his heart to forgive the prodigal and welcome him back?"

We ask not only why Peter denied his Lord but also why he was given the power to become a disciple of the risen Christ. We ask not only, "Why do we sin and 'fall short of the glory of God'?" (Rom. 3:23) but also ask, "Why does Christ die for us 'while we [are yet] sinners'?" (Rom. 5:8). The issue is whether we focus primarily on the perplexing existence of sin and suffering or upon the immeasurable riches of God's grace. The scope of our questioning may determine whether we become trapped in despair or set free by joy.

What is our dominant question? Is it, "Why is there so much tragedy?" or "How can there be so much grace?"

Are you ready now to ask, "Why, God, why?" from a completely different perspective and with a completely different tone? Will you ask God "Why?" not only for your tragedies but also for your blessings? Will you remember to ask God how it is that you deserve the good things that have happened to you?

Identical questions may have a very different attitude behind them. I might ask, "What did I do to deserve my parents?" But I would raise that question from a different perspective than a child who suffered from parental abuse. But no matter how difficult our life situation has been, there still have been positive gifts from life and from God. What good things have come your way? What have you done to deserve them? As you think of them will you ask, "Why, God, why?"

Some ask: "What did I do to deserve loving parents?" "Why, God, was I able to find a loving spouse or a faithful friend?" "Why, God, should I have food and shelter and luxuries when so many in our world suffer with little or nothing? What did I do to deserve this?" "How could I be so lucky as to have been born in the United States?" "What did I do to deserve living in the South after air conditioning instead of before it?" "What did I do to deserve a computer that saves my rough drafts and allows me to correct my sermons in a fraction of the time that it took the founders of the church? Why, God, was I allowed to experience the nurture of people in the church? Is it fair? What have I done to deserve it?"

> *"Why, God, was I allowed to experience the nurture of people in the church?"*

We all could raise not one but hundreds of "Why, God, why?" questions if we took time to reflect. And just as we do not deserve many of the bad things that happen to us, we do not deserve many of the good things that come our way.

We need to be fair in our questioning: "When sorrow

comes, we have no right to ask, 'Why did this happen to me?' unless we ask the same question whenever joy comes our way." [2]

In his letter to the church at Philippi, Paul gives several astounding instructions to these young Christians. Most amazing is his instruction to "Rejoice in the Lord always . . ." (Phil. 4:4*a*). Doesn't Paul ever ask that most basic of questions: "Why, God, why?" Didn't Paul have reason to question life's fairness? You decide whether Paul's life made it hard for him to rejoice always, whether he had cause to ask, "Why, God, why?" He writes of some of his ordeals:

> Five times I have received from the Jews the forty lashes minus one. Three times I was beaten with rods. Once I received a stoning. Three times I was shipwrecked; for a night and a day I was adrift at sea; on frequent journeys, in danger from rivers, danger from bandits, danger from my own people, danger from Gentiles, danger in the city, danger in the wilderness, danger at sea, danger from false brothers and sisters; in toil and hardship, through many a sleepless night, hungry and thirsty, often without food, cold and naked. (2 Cor. 11:24-27)

Aren't these grounds for asking the agonizing question, "Why, God, why?" I think so. Paul's list of hardships certainly makes my complaining about my eczema and car problems seem minor by comparison!

Paul was not obsessed with asking, "Why, God, why?" of his trying circumstances. But he must have asked why he should be so richly blessed. He must have asked why God would choose him to be an apostle, to have the special privilege of sharing the truth of the gospel with the Gentiles. He must have been grateful for God's empowering him to do the work he was assigned. He must have felt grateful that one who had persecuted the Christians could be forgiven and allowed to be a part of the Christian fellowship.

The ultimate question for Paul was not, "Why is there sin and suffering and tragedy?" A prior question for Paul was, "Why, God, should we receive all this marvelous grace?" So this man who suffered much could move from questions of why to an attitude of thanksgiving and shouts of praise. This man who suffered from the "thorn in his side" could invite the church at Philippi to join with him in praise:

> Rejoice in the Lord always; again I will say, Rejoice. . . . Do not worry about anything, but in everything by prayer and supplication with thanksgiving let your requests be made known to God. And the peace of God, which surpasses all understanding, will guard your hearts and your minds in Christ Jesus.   (Phil. 4:4, 6-7)

Perhaps you and I do not ask, "Why, God, why?" too often. Perhaps we ask the question too seldom.

Perhaps you and I do not ask, "Why, God, why?" too often. Perhaps we ask the question too seldom. Maybe we can agree to a rule for its usage: "When sorrow comes, we have no right to ask, 'Why did this happen to me?' unless we ask the same question whenever joy comes our way."

> *His disciples asked him, "Rabbi, who sinned, this man or his parents, that he was born blind?" John 9:2*
>
> *He asked them, "Do you think that because these Galileans suffered in this way they were worse sinners than all other Galileans?" Luke 13:2*

God of Pain or Compassion?

For countless centuries, people have been lifting their voices of despair or confusion: "Why, God, why?" "Why was my baby deformed?" "Why did the earthquake destroy the city?" "Why am I sick?" "Why did that accident have to happen?"

In the face of almost every tragedy, hardship, or sickness, people have asked, why. "Is there any reason for these things to happen?" In the Old Testament, one interpretation seems to dominate the others: tragedy, catastrophe, sickness, defeat are often understood as direct actions of God. These devastations are seen as a means of God's punishment for sin. According to this theological position, the root cause of suffering is sin. If one is sick, it is because of the spiritual unfaithfulness of the person.

Throughout much of the Old Testament, hardship and suffering are understood as tools of God—tools to punish, chastise, test, or temper the people of God. Suffering,

tragedy, and hardship often were not understood as occur-
ring by chance or as a result of human error; they were
seen simply as God's intervention in response to the sins
of the people. It is ironic that many insurance policies still
refer to hurricanes, tornadoes, and earthquakes as "acts of
God." I wonder: Is this the kind of God we worship?

Jesus was quite aware of the prevailing theology of his
day. Sickness still was understood as a manifestation of sinfulness. Material wealth, health, large families often were
seen as signs of God's approval. But many people still were
not convinced of such a theology. Many who witnessed
their own suffering and the suffering of others continued
to raise the probing question: "Why?" "Why do people suffer? Is it really because of sin? If so, whose sin?"

The sermon texts raise these existential dilemmas. In
John, we hear the question of Jesus' disciples as they
observe a blind man: "Rabbi, who sinned, this man or his
parents that he was born blind?" (John 9:2b). Jesus did not
give an orthodox answer. He did not draw any connection
at all between the man's sinfulness and his predicament. In
fact, Jesus eliminates this theology altogether. He says,
"Neither this man nor his parents sinned" (John 9:3a).

Likewise, in the Gospel of Luke, we find Jesus taking a
similar stand. This time the circumstance is not a personal
affliction but a major disaster. Jesus asks the rhetorical
question: "Those eighteen who were killed when the tower
of Siloam fell on them—do you think that they were worse
offenders than all the others living in Jerusalem?" Jesus
answers his own question with an emphatic "No" (Luke
13:4, 5a). Jesus is suggesting that in the face of disaster,
tragedy, or sickness, one cannot draw conclusions as to the
"goodness or wickedness" of the victims. Jesus would have
us reject the notion that tragedy is to be understood as a
punishment for wrongdoing.

This is not to say that tragedy cannot be a direct result

of our wrongdoing or poor judgment. We can smoke cigarettes for thirty years and then develop lung cancer. Such a disease is not the punishment for sin but rather the consequence of harmful habits. It is the body's reaction to abuse. At the end of our lives we may face financial ruin or poor health, all because of our behavior and lifestyle.

> *Sin does have consequences.*

Sin does have consequences. Evil *does* entrap us in various tragedies: loss of friends, lack of meaning, backlash, resentment, and hostility. But the question raised today is not whether or not we may suffer from our own sinfulness; indeed, all sin causes suffering!

The basic question we are facing today is whether or not the suffering we experience should be understood as a punishment from God. Such a question is not one limited to biblical times. I have heard several parishioners with severe illnesses say, "I must have been a bad person to have to suffer like this." Others tearfully question, "What have I done to deserve this?"—as if to say, "God is doing this to me. Why?"

Jesus never fully answers the question of why. He does not give us an adequate reason for our suffering. What Jesus does instead is to suffer with us, for us, like us. Jesus has experienced what we now experience. Jesus knows what suffering means. He now suffers with us.

In reflecting upon suffering, Jesus is quick to rule out one theological premise. He refutes the idea that all tragedy, sickness, and hardship are punishment for sin.

Jesus would never want us to assume that if someone suffers a deep human tragedy that such is a sign of deep sinfulness.

> *He refutes the idea that all tragedy, sickness, and hardship are punishment for sin.*

And don't we all know of experiences in life that support this truth? Don't we all know saints who have suffered greatly? Don't we know scoundrels who seem to hardly suffer at all? If anything, I am inclined to conclude that the good people of this world seem to suffer the most. And of this I am certain: The truly good people of this earth are able to suffer and still not be defeated.

The choice before us is to decide whether we have a God of pain or a God of compassion, whether we believe in a God who inflicts pain to punish or change us, or a God who sends rain on the just and unjust and allows tragedy to fall on the good and the bad.

My hunch is that some of us make God a God of punishment because of our own guilt. Several years ago I visited with a woman who had faced one major crisis after another. I honestly did not know how she could handle all the problems, suffering, and anxiety. But I was surprised one day when she said she wondered if God was punishing her for her wrongdoing.

My first impulse was to say God does not act that way, instead I decided to ask a question. "Have you done anything in your life that you think is deserving of your present suffering?" Before she realized it, and before I was prepared for it, she confessed to a serious wrongdoing.

I do not believe that God was punishing her for her wrongdoing. God was not causing problems for members of her family as a means of divine punishment or as a motivation for her to change her behavior. Rather, she was so burdened by her guilt that she felt deserving of God's judgment. Perhaps she even wanted God or someone to somehow force her to stop.

Most of us, if we were given God's absolute power for a day, would do things differently. Many of us would ensure quick justice. Thieves would have their loot snatched from their hands. Criminals would not have trials but instant punishment, because with divine powers we could determine unmistakably who was guilty and who was innocent. We might even give some reward to those who were nice—perhaps better health, a bonus of some sort.

We might rig the lotteries to pay only to those who would be generous with their winnings. We might bless all the churchgoers and place a mild affliction on those who choose not to worship. If we were allowed to be God and have God's power, things probably would be different. Goodness would be instantly rewarded and evil would be readily and firmly punished. And it would be a better world.

Several years ago I would have especially enjoyed having supernatural powers. A young man liked to ride his motorcycle with no muffler through the apartment complex where we lived—especially in the middle of the night! As he neared our window he would slow down to avoid the speed bumps, then rack the pipes, thus awakening half of the apartment complex. He avoided the speed bumps by riding through the small gap in the middle that was just wide enough for his small tires.

I must confess to fantasizing about putting tacks in that gap or a wire or rope across the road, even though I knew that might be dangerous. But what a thrill it would have been to possess the divine power to yank him off his bike and drop him in the countryside where he would be forced to walk home!

If we could be God, we would probably reward goodness and punish evil. But under that system, how could one ever be truly good? If being good were always to our advantage, could we ever really act unselfishly? Could we ever really sacrifice solely for the sake of others?

> *Good is neither always immediately rewarded nor evil always resisted or conquered.*

Today, God is still in charge. Yet there is still suffering, even undeserved suffering. How then do we understand God's role? Is God the instrument of pain or the instrument of comfort? Paul gives a partial answer to this question in his letter to the church at Corinth: "Blessed be the God and Father of our Lord Jesus Christ, the Father of mercies and the God of all consolation, who consoles us in all our affliction, so that we may be able to console those who are in any affliction with the consolation with which we ourselves are consoled by God" (2 Cor. 1:3-4).

I suggest along with Paul that God is not the cause of suffering, but its healer. God is not the creator of pain, but rather the one who hears our cries and offers the presence of the Holy Spirit. God is not constantly slapping our hands, but lovingly offering to walk with us. God is not forever giving out rewards, but instead offers us his guidance through the Spirit and the Word.

By now, surely we have realized that life is not fair. It does not ensure equality. There is no exact justice. Good is neither always immediately rewarded nor evil always resisted or conquered.

Our God comes not to give us pain but to be with us in our pain. God comes as our comforter and invites us to be a part of the healing process. We can comfort others as God comforts them. We can offer our prayers, our cards, our food, our help, our presence. We cannot take the pain away, but we can help others to bear it.

Christians are not ones who are protected from all pain. Rather, Christians are given an antidote. We are given the presence of God, a presence that can offer us power, spiritual healing, and peace.

In my ministry, I have witnessed people in the midst of pain and suffering who have received God's healing presence even in the face of death. I know that these spiritual healings happen. The God I worship is not one who brings suffering to us. Instead, the God I worship offers us loving presence. My understanding of God is like the one Paul describes in 2 Corinthians.

He comes not to punish. He comes to comfort those who suffer. "Blessed be the God and Father of our Lord Jesus Christ, the Father of mercies and the God of all consolation, who consoles us in all our affliction, so that we may be able to console those who are in any affliction with the consolation with which we ourselves are consoled by God" (2 Cor. 1:3-4). So may we all be comforted! So may we all give comfort!

> *We know that all things work together for good for those who love God, who are called according to his purpose. Romans 8:28*

Everything Working for Good?

I n Romans 8:28, Paul makes perhaps the most daring claim of his ministry! It is a claim he makes not only for himself but also on behalf of the Christians in Rome. Some would argue he even speaks for us when he says, "We know that all things work together for good for those who love God, who are called according to his purpose."

Do we know that in everything God works for good? Are we willing to join in Paul's outlandish claim? Are we willing to defend this position to those who stand outside the faith? Can we proclaim to others, "No matter how bad things seem right now, God will work with you to see that things work out for good"? Is this just wishful thinking or is it gospel?

Can we defend God's ability to resurrect good out of tragedy, injustice, evil acts, failure, natural disaster, betrayal, child abuse, sickness and death? Is God able to bring good out of these terrible circumstances? Paul says, "all things work together for good. . . ." This is not to say that God causes all things to happen. This is not to say that God wills all things. This is not to suggest that everything that happens is for the best. On the contrary, Paul's position suggests that even when things are not as they should be, even when things happen that are counter to the will of God, even when things are tragic, even when things are teeming with pain and suffering, God is active while we are discovering good in the midst of these experiences. And God empowers us to discern that good.

> *"We know that all things work together for good for those who love God, who are called according to his purpose."*

God, then, is not merely an intervenor or protector but an active partner in our struggles and crises. God neither bestows on us the pain of human tragedy to teach us a lesson nor gives us hardship to force us to grow. Rather, God is present with us in these times of trial to ensure that we grow and have hope sufficient for our challenges.

God does not ignite the fires that threaten to destroy us. Rather, God helps us fight the flames. And when great tragedy comes, God stoops down to help us sift through the ashes to discover treasures—things we can take with us from that experience as we begin anew.

Without Paul's daring claim, we are left with no word of encouragement for those who suffer tragic human loss. Without the gift of God's help, many would be left with the poor alternatives of bitterness, despair, self-pity, cynicism, and no faith.

But the question remains for us: "Can we affirm Paul's claim?" Can we believe it is true for us and will be true for those who suffer far more than we? Can we say with voices of faith that in everything God works for good?

Most of us have learned from life's experiences that, in retrospect, many things that were traumatic at a particular time in our lives have proved to be opportunities for great good:

- a job that we did not get—and a better one came later;
- a romantic relationship that ended and later was seen as a dead-end street;
- a time of illness that helped bring a better perspective on life;
- a personal failure that brought new compassion and genuine humility.

In retrospect, many things that were traumatic at a particular time in our lives have proved to be opportunities for great good.

All of us could give personal examples of some experience in our past that seemed tragic at the time but later brought blessings to us. Perhaps in some cases those experiences were even worth the pain and suffering for the good they brought.

Each of us can readily affirm that some things have worked for good, even those things that have brought us pain. Perhaps even some of the things that initially brought us the greatest harm have provided the greatest gain. But Paul is even more daring in his assertion. He is not claiming that only *some* things have potential for good but that *all* things have the potential for good. Further, he does not claim that good *may* come out of it but that good *will* come out of it, at least to those who love God. Paul asserts that the key change agent is God. God, in partnership with us, helps resurrect light out of darkness, hope out of despair, good things out of the dregs of human tragedy.

I appreciate the way the New English Bible translates this verse: "In everything, as we know, [God] co-operates for good with those who love God. . . ." Paul has made a very bold claim about life and about God's interaction in life. Is Paul trustworthy? Would you buy a used car from Paul? Does Paul know what he is talking about? Has Paul had enough bad things happen to him to validate his theological position?

Here is Paul's account in 2 Corinthians:

> Three times I was beaten with rods. Once I received a stoning. Three times I was shipwrecked; for a night and a day I was adrift at sea; on frequent journeys, in danger from rivers, danger from bandits, danger from my own people, danger from Gentiles, danger in the city, danger in the wilderness, danger at sea, danger from false brothers and sisters; in toil and hardship, through many a sleepless night, hungry and thirsty, often without food, cold and naked. (2 Cor. 11:25-27)

What do you think? If Paul says, "In *all things* God works for good," has his premise been fully tested? Can we believe him when he insists that even through pain and suffering God can always resurrect good things?

Paul is not the only figure in the Bible who believed in such an idea. Joseph of the Old Testament certainly reflects the same notion when he speaks of his trials and tribulations. Joseph, who was betrayed by his brothers, thrown into a pit, sold into slavery, persecuted because of his moral scruples, and forgotten by those he befriended, was able to say concerning the tragic events of his life: "[When others] intended to do harm to me, God intended it for good" (Gen. 50:20).

God did not throw Joseph into the pit, but God did help

Joseph make the best of it. God did not coax Joseph's brothers into acts of betrayal, but God was able to transform their acts of jealousy into an opportunity to fight famine in a time of draught.

We all could give stories to support Paul's thesis—if not personal ones, then ones of friends, family, or acquaintances—stories that proclaim that God works for good even in tragic circumstances.

Have some of us not seen painful divorces that ended with happy second marriages, personal tragedy that mobilized the love and support of family and friends, or prolonged illness that offered time to sort things out and time to get priorities in proper order?

Most of us believe that good *may* come out of almost any situation. We have witnessed such surprising happenings. We know that good is possible, but often we don't know how. So in the face of tragedy or crisis we may try our best to think positive thoughts, but we often lack a deep faith in Paul's promise.

Every day one or more of us will be confronted with a real test of Paul's daring claim. At that time we may want to confront Paul, "Tell me, sir, what good can come out of this?"

What possible good could come out of the death of a premature baby? the miscarriage of justice? the abuse of a marriage partner? What possible good could be served by the tragedies of war? the onset of Alzheimer's the tragic murder of an innocent bystander?

Circumstances such as these test our faith when they involve us personally or even when we simply read their tragic accounts in the newspapers. In any case, I would not suggest that we start telling those who suffer to look for a silver lining. That would sound trite and uncaring to the ones who are hurting. This is a message that must be realized from within. Paul is asking us to accept in our minds and hearts that in everything that happens *to us*, no matter how tragic or painful, God will *work with us* to bring about ultimate good.

We can learn to trust in God even when our vision is blurred, even when we can see only darkness, even when we feel only immense pain. In the darkest night of our soul we are asked to believe in the daybreak of God's grace.

We are asked to believe the unbelievable—that in absolutely everything God works for good!

> *In the darkest night of our soul we are asked to believe in the daybreak of God's grace.*

But we have one important point yet to explore. It is the part of this verse that I have never really wanted to acknowledge. It is the part that says, ". . . for those who love God." I don't like the way that sounds! It sounds at first as though God is willing to work for good only with those who love him. It sounds like favoritism!

But I do not believe that is what this passage means. Scripture tells us that God sends rain on the just and on the unjust. God has never really played favorites with people. Ask the Hebrews! If God played favorites with them, then pity God's enemies!

No, the reason things work for good only to those who love God is not because God does not offer good things to all but because some refuse God's help. God cannot help people discover the good in all things if they respond in bitterness and self-pity. God cannot give a new dawn to one who hides in the shadowy cave of despair.

Paul's daring claim is a matter of choice. We either believe that God has the power to work good in the midst of all circumstances or we do not believe. Sometimes we believe because we can see the potential good. Sometimes we believe because we have previously experienced such grace. Sometimes we trust in some good outcome because we believe in a loving and powerful God, a God who will not idly stand by while we suffer.

As Christians we have been given evidence enough of God's power to bring good out of evil, hope out of despair, life out of death. Have we not all heard of the cross? Are we not the people of the resurrection? Do we not know stories of people like Viktor Frankl, Helen Keller? Have we not seen green shoots come out of dry stumps, new life from weary friends, fireweed in the midst of burned forests?

The opportunities to examine our belief in God's providence and grace are endless. Life will test our creed as surely as it tested Paul's. We will be "shipwrecked and beaten." Most certainly we will suffer!

Yet, will our faith mature so that we will always believe in God's power to bring good out of all things? Will we continue to profess that God works in all things for good to those who dare to believe in his power and who seek his grace?

The cantata titled "Melodious Accord" by Alice Parker was based on the words of a hymn written by William Cowper. Of the various pieces in this composition none is more touching than the closing number that was based on a familiar hymn. The words seem to be a restatement of Paul's message to the church at Rome. I invite you to embrace its message:

> God moves in a mysterious way
> His wonders to perform;
> He plants his footsteps in the sea,
> And rides upon the storm.
> Deep in unfathomable mines
> Of never-failing skill

He treasures up his bright designs,
And works his sovereign will.

Ye fearful saints, fresh courage take;
The clouds ye so much dread
Are big with mercy, and shall break
In blessings on your head.

Judge not the Lord by feeble sense,
But trust him for his grace;
Behind a frowning providence
He hides a smiling face.

Blind unbelief is sure to err,
And scan his work in vain;
God is his own interpreter,
And he will make it plain.[3]

Paul was right: "We know that all things work together for good for those who love God, who are called according to his purpose."

> *If we confess our sins, he who is faithful and just will forgive us our sins and cleanse us from all unrighteousness.* 1 John 1:9

Bad News, Good News!

I have some good news and some bad news. Let's start with the bad news—there is plenty of that to go around. Media coverage has given us much bad news of late: continuing military conflict around our world, violence in our streets, racial strife in our own community. We are inundated by bad news.

But all of these particular tragedies were avoidable; they are the result of the misuse of human freedom. They reflect in part the sinfulness of our world and our need for God's forgiveness and power.

Most of us do not understand the violence that is going on in our world. We lament the needless loss of human lives. As Christians we grope for ways to address the root causes of violence and conflict.

But part of the bad news that I share with you is not restricted to the rest of the world. Part of the bad news is that WE ourselves are sinful. We contribute to the bad news of our world. Maybe our sinfulness does not make headlines, but it still takes its toll on us and on those around us.

The sermon text from 1 John is very straightforward. It

says, "If we say that we have no sin, we deceive ourselves, and the truth is not in us" (1 John 1:8).

That's bad news: we are sinners! That's bad news for us, bad news for our world, and bad news for God!

The New Testament repeats this theme of our common sinfulness not once but many, many times. In our Gospel text we are told the story of Jesus' interaction with the crowd gathered to stone the woman who had been caught in the act of adultery. They knew she was "bad news." They were quick to condemn her and quite willing to carry out the Mosaic sentence of death by stoning. Jesus did not have to challenge the validity of the Mosaic law in order to save her life. He used a different tactic to disarm them.

> *"If we say that we have no sin, we deceive ourselves, and the truth is not in us." (1 John 1:8)*

He told them to proceed but placed a simple condition upon their act of strict justice. He told them: "Let anyone among you who is without sin be the first to throw a stone at her"(John 8:7*b*). But even among such a pious and righteous crowd no one stepped forward. One by one they dropped their stones and walked away.

Everyone felt righteous enough to condemn her, but no one felt innocent enough to cast the first stone. They all agreed with Jesus' assumption: none in the crowd was without sin. Only Jesus could have carried out the sentence. Only Jesus who was without sin could cast the first stone, but he chose mercy. Do we fault him?

Paul, in his letter to the church at Rome, shared with the young congregation the bad news: "All have sinned and fall short of the glory of God" (Rom. 3:23). Our tendency today is to break Paul's words into two parts and then to reinterpret them. We would like to believe that what Paul meant was this: "*Others* are truly sinful! *We* simply fall short of God's glory!" We would like to think there are only two types of people: sinners and the righteous! (By the way, do you have any idea which group you belong to?)

> *Everyone felt righteous enough to condemn her, but no one felt innocent enough to cast the first stone.*

But Paul's statement is not multiple choice or mix and match. We *all* have sinned and thus *all* have fallen short of God's glory. The bad news is not just that there is sin, and that tragedies occur with the misuse of human freedom. The bad news is that *we* are part of the problem: we *all* are sinners! None of us is innocent. None of us has any business carrying stones in our hands; we will never be able to use them!

But the bad news is not limited to our being sinners. The bad news is that we now fall into the same category with terrorists and deranged cult leaders and criminals and abusers—wretched sinners of the world. We are not granted separate living quarters labeled "home of the righteous." We are not set apart as those who need no repentance. We are in the same dinghy with all those who are unworthy of God's grace.

We spend too much of our time evaluating the worth of others. We waste our time trying to divide everyone into two groups: those who need God's mercy and those who can stand on their own merits. Perhaps we divide people in our minds: the lazy ones and we diligent ones; the wasteful ones and we frugal ones; the violent ones and we peace-loving folk; the criminals and we law-abiding citizens. We try to finish our careful work of dividing God's people so that we finally have two distinct groups: the truly sinful and the almost totally good. To put it another way—two groups: the unacceptable and those who are a little less than perfect.

I've got some bad news for us: We all are in the same boat. We all are sinners. We all fall short of the glory of God. There are not two groups but one.

Jesus made certain that none of us could claim to be perfect. He increased the requirements for moral goodness. In the Sermon on the Mount, Jesus made clear that not only our outward actions are judged but also our inner thoughts and motives.

Never committed adultery? Okay, Jesus now asks a tougher question: Have you ever fantasized adultery? Have you ever lusted? If so, Jesus suggests that you have committed adultery in your heart (Matt. 5:27-28). Ever killed someone? No? I didn't think so! Have you ever called someone a fool? Have you ever wished someone harm in your heart? If so, you are not innocent (Matt. 5:22).

Need I go on? Is everyone convicted now? I know I am. Or are there still a few saintly ones untouched? If you still believe you are innocent and truly good, I ask you this additional question: Do you pray for your enemies (Matt. 5:43-44)? Have you forgiven those who have hurt you? Have you learned always to have thanksgiving in your heart? Have you avoided jealousy and envy when others received something you wanted for yourself? Are we all guilty now?

Jesus' demands make it impossible for us to gain the right to stone others. His logic is simple: none of us is without sin. There is no need to further subdivide humankind. We all need God's forgiveness. There is no need to suggest that some need it more than others.

We all are sinners. Bad news! Very bad news! So what could be news good enough to overcome that? The words of 1 John bring us that special good news: "If we confess our sins, [God] who is faithful and just and will forgive our sins and cleanse us from all unrighteousness" (1 John 1:9).

Is that good news or not? We can be forgiven even though we are sinners, sometimes terrible sinners. In fact, everyone can be forgiven! Are we still happy? There is only one thing that might spoil our good news: What if we don't want God to forgive everybody? What if the "good news" becomes "bad news" when God forgives our enemy?

Would God forgive a cult leader like David Koresh if he truly confessed his sin? Would God forgive an abusive father, an unfaithful husband, a vindictive wife? Would God spare those who have done terrible deeds if they truly confessed and repented?

Is God's mercy and forgiveness good news or bad news? Are you happy enough with forgiveness offered to you that you will not pout when others also receive it? Will you be surprised at the people you see in heaven—as surprised as they will be to see you and me?

> *Let us drop our stones and take bread in its place— living bread, the bread that symbolizes Christ's body and the unbelievable forgiveness he promised.*

Our world is filled with bad news. You don't have to read the paper or watch TV. Tragedy occurs in our own community. People get sick. Some die. Injustice takes place in business, government, families, schools, churches. People get hurt by the cruelty of others.

But in the midst of all the bad news, the gospel brings us

the good news: courage in the face of trouble, comfort in the midst of sorrow, faith with the erosion of doubt, hope in the midst of despair.

But perhaps the greatest good news of all is the astonishing surprise of forgiveness. How can Jesus offer forgiveness to the adulterer? How can God forgive the terrorist? How can our Creator forgive those who so often think themselves better than others? How can God forgive both the prodigal son and the elder brother?

I don't know why or even how God forgives such sinners, but I do believe his promise, a promise that is amazingly good news! God's promise means that all of us can leave this place today as forgiven people. No matter what we've done, even with all the pain we've caused others, we can be forgiven. We need not worry about the fate of our brother or sister for the moment. For now, we are the ones in need of forgiveness.

So as we come to the Lord's table to partake of Holy Communion, let us drop our stones and take bread in its place—living bread, the bread that symbolizes Christ's body and the unbelievable forgiveness he promised.

Hear again the bad news and then the good news:

"All have sinned and fall short of the glory of God" (Rom. 3:23). "If we confess our sins, he who is faithful and just will forgive us our sins and cleanse us from all unrighteousness" (1 John 1:9). We come to the table as sinners. We leave as Christ's forgiven people! Thanks be to God! Amen.

> *But we have this treasure in earthen vessels, to show that the transcendent power belongs to God and not to us. We are afflicted in every way, but not crushed; perplexed, but not driven to despair; persecuted, but not forsaken; struck down, but not destroyed.* 2 Corinthians 4:7-9 *(RSV)*

Earthen Vessels

This sermon is a narrative. The text will be illustrated through the wrestlings of a young woman that I will call Susan. Some might argue that Susan never existed, that her story is neither believable nor true. But I have known many Susans. In fact, I have even felt like Susan at various times in my life. You may be certain, Susan is real!

Some who hear the story may think Susan's life is too tragic, too depressing. But others find in her journey much hope. They are encouraged, "If Susan can find the answer to life maybe there is hope for me. Maybe I, too, can find inner peace."

Susan's childhood was rather typical. She went through the terrible twos, the defiant fives and nines; then before her parents could say "bobby socks" Susan was a teenager, listening to Elvis and Pat Boone, trying to discover who she was.

Her teenage years were fairly difficult because Susan was plagued by gnawing fears—fears of being rejected, hurt, or ignored. She often found herself following the crowd even while questioning their behavior. She wanted to be accepted. Surely nothing could be worse than being rejected by her peers!

What Susan wanted was something she could grab hold of, something that would make her feel secure. She wondered if it would be better if she were a guy. The guys she knew didn't seem to have fears or act so insecure.

Susan made it through high school and college with the normal amount of emotional scars. Most of the traumatic experiences were short-lived romances, but she eventually learned how to keep from becoming too involved. She set her sights on something that would be sure to pay off. She started working toward a career.

When Susan landed a good job right out of college, she expected to finally feel good about herself, but she continued to be haunted by her fears. Susan wanted something solid in her life. She wanted a sense of security, a "piece of the rock." So Susan did the sensible thing: she contacted her Prudential agent, but with no positive results. The next day E. F. Hutton called; Susan listened, but again nothing developed.

During the spring of 1966 Susan's life took a dramatic turn. She dressed herself in a gorgeous white dress with a long train, walked down a red-carpeted aisle and said "I do" in front of two hundred people.

Surely marriage would bring Susan the happiness and security she had always wanted! The new beginning sparked a hope within her that she would find stability for her life and that her nagging fears would finally leave.

Marriage did bring a special joy to her life. Her husband, Jim, was a friend before he was her husband. They had been coworkers in a large computer firm. Their marriage showed great promise! They had so much in common! They both wanted financial security! They both wanted to wait before starting a family, and they both loved jamoca almond fudge ice cream. It was a marriage made in heaven!

Susan expected great things of her marriage—perhaps too much. She expected her husband to provide the piece of the puzzle that had always been missing in her life. She wanted him to dispel her fears, be her rock, provide the emotional security she desperately needed.

As the years passed, Susan's fears and sense of loneliness increased. She could not understand why she was so unhappy. They both had good jobs. They both ate right, got plenty of rest, and took vitamins every day. But, even so, her life seemed as fragile as it had been in her teen years. Somehow she knew there must be something more.

Susan decided to turn to the church—nothing fanatical, you understand. She managed to go to worship about twice a month. Jim stayed home and read the Sunday paper.

On one particular Sunday, Susan went with high hopes. She had read the title of the sermon in the church newspaper: "A Firm Foundation for Our Shaky Lives!" "That was certainly a sermon meant for me !" she thought. Susan listened intently to the message. The minister talked of hope, faith, and caring. He suggested that we must get beyond preoccupation with ourselves.

> *We must get beyond preoccupation with ourselves.*

Some of what the preacher said made sense, but Susan was disappointed that her life took no turn for the better. She was so weary of the turmoil and uncertainty. She wanted a reason for living! Gradually she went less and less often to church and finally quit altogether. Maybe she would find her answer elsewhere!

Within a few years, Susan experienced one of life's biggest little miracles. Susan gave birth to a screaming eight-pound, seven-ounce baby boy. For a while Susan forgot about her search. How content she was just to hold baby Jason in her arms! She was no longer alone. Susan enjoyed physical touch, delightful smiles, and a sense of purpose. At last she had a reason for being!

But Jason did not remain a cuddly infant. The time flew by! Early on he cooed and listened. Later he began to talk —then talk back. And at the magic age of twelve his home vocabulary shrank to ten words, with two of his favorites being "huh?" and "yuk!"

During Jason's early teen years Susan's fears and insecurity returned in full force. She was afraid she was failing as a mother. Failing as a wife was already an ever-present probability. Jim had mentioned a trial separation.

Things were getting progressively worse. Instead of feeling more in control of her life with each passing year, Susan felt more and more helpless.

She was losing hope about ever finding a foundation on which to build her life; and was beginning to believe her best course might well be to become a rock herself—to commit herself to a detached hardness, to protect herself from feeling and involvement. Susan began to ask herself, "What else could go wrong?" One word of advice: don't ever ask "What else can go wrong?"

> *Instead of feeling more in control of her life, she felt more helpless.*

Jason began to have difficulty in school. He started running around with the wrong crowd and occasionally getting into trouble. Her marriage wasn't doing well either. On Susan's fortieth birthday, Jim took her out to dinner and after dessert presented her with divorce papers.

The divorce was rough on Susan but at least the negotiations were civil. Susan was given custody of Jason. The financial settlement was quite generous.

The only real surprise was that Susan felt no lonelier after the divorce than before. As the weeks passed she became better acquainted with someone she had long needed to know. She began to discover herself for the first time. And in the midst of her pain she again wondered if there was a solution to her longing for peace and wholeness.

Once again Susan tried the church, but this time she decided to worship regularly and become a part of a small group. There was no immediate filling of the void within her, but she did start hoping again.

> *In the midst of her pain she again wondered if there was a solution to her longing for peace and wholeness.*

Like a swimmer coming out of deep water, Susan thrust down her feet of faith, hoping to strike something solid, hoping to find a foundation on which to stand. She was so tired of treading water. She was weary of feeling vulnerable and afraid.

Then one day Susan's life took a radical turn. Susan was given the startling news—she had a rare liver disease. The doctor told her she probably had less than a year to live. For the first time in her life, the focus of Susan's fears changed. She had always worried about herself. She had always been concerned about *her* friends, *her* marriage, *her* sense of accomplishment, *her* ability to control things, *her* vulnerability.

But on the day the doctor dropped this bombshell, Susan's fears refused to focus primarily on herself. Susan remembered her teenage fears and the loneliness. She could not fathom the idea that Jason would be left alone.

Susan was so afraid for Jason, she hardly thought of her own fears. All her life she had been concerned about her own vulnerability. She had never fully realized that others were vulnerable, too.

During the next nine months Susan did a lot of thinking, a lot of praying. She even read a black leather book with gold edges. She was amazed at the promises and images it contained. The words were like therapy for the soul.

But Susan's body continued to deteriorate. During the next several months Susan suffered a great amount of pain but she told almost everyone who visited her, "I couldn't have chosen a better way to die. A heart attack would have been too quick for me. I'm more dense than most people. I had to learn the hard way about fear and security, storms and peace."

As Susan faced the early weeks of her illness, Matthew 7:24-25 became a key passage for her. She read the words over and over:

> Everyone then who hears these words of mine and acts on them will be like a wise man who built his house on rock. The rain fell, the floods came, and the winds blew and beat on that house, but it did not fall, because it had been founded on rock.

"One who hears Jesus' words and does them—I guess that means loving," she thought to herself. "I guess that means trusting in God. I guess that means giving up the idea that we can build our own security."

> *"I couldn't have chosen a better way to die. A heart attack would have been too quick for me. I'm more dense than most people. I had to learn the hard way about fear and security, storms and peace."*

Susan smiled as she closed her Bible. Life seemed so different now. Things were the worst they had ever been, yet strangely better. She only wished she had understood earlier.

Susan's greatest breakthrough came only a few months before her death. She had been reading straight through the New Testament. She had already read the Gospels, Acts, Romans, and 1 Corinthians. She was reading in 2 Corinthians, when two words suddenly leaped from the page.

How simple it all was now! "Earthen vessels!" We have this treasure in "earthen vessels." That's it! We are vulnerable! All of us! Every last one of us!

Susan rubbed her eyes; the tears were blurring her vision. She read again those powerful words of Paul:

> But we have this treasure in earthen vessels, to show that the transcendent power belongs to God and not to us. We are afflicted in every way, but not crushed; persecuted, but not forsaken; struck down, but not destroyed. (2 Cor. 4:7-9 RSV)

"Why have I always understood vulnerability as weakness?" she thought to herself. "Why did I turn to myself and to empty promises when I could have turned to God and the glorious promises of the Word?"

Susan had spent a lifetime trying to protect her "earthen vessels." She had tried to protect herself from the storms of life through her own efforts. But storms are bigger and more powerful than our fragile defenses; our vessels are sure to crack or break.

Susan and Jason talked a lot during those last few months. Susan had great hopes for Jason and only moderate fear about his future. She no longer worried about what lay ahead of her. Susan had finally found her rock.

When the end came, Susan passed serenely from peace into peace. She was led by a Loving Shepherd from abundant life into a realm that knows no end.

Jason smiled through his tears as he placed flowers on his mother's grave. All the friends and relatives were waiting down the road. Jason might have been embarrassed if others could see his faint smile. But his mother would understand.

Jason was sorrowful and at that moment even a bit angry at God. But he was also grateful. Susan had given him many great gifts. She had given him her love and her recent hope. She had shared with him the secret of "earthen vessels."

At sixteen Jason was just beginning to understand what had eluded Susan for almost forty-four years. He now knew that we are all vulnerable. We can be battered, hurt, betrayed. Life teaches us: earthen vessels are destined to break. But Jason had also come to believe that when they break, there is a power, a transcendent power, offered to us!

Jason arranged the potted flowers on his mother's grave. It was their secret symbol—two cracked clay pots at the foot of her grave, two pots with yellow mums bursting into full bloom.

Jason now shared Susan's priceless discovery. But Susan's witness of faith had first been Paul's witness to the church at Corinth: "We have this treasure in earthen vessels to show that the transcendent power belongs to God and not to us" (2 Cor. 4:7 RSV).

> *Therefore, to keep me from being too elated, a thorn was given me in the flesh, a messenger of Satan to torment me, to keep me from being too elated.* 2 Corinthians 12:7b

Blessed Thorn!

*I*n his letter to the church at Corinth, Paul comes dangerously close to giving thanks for something he called a "thorn in the flesh." Though he did not welcome the thorn, Paul admitted that he had benefited from it. He said that it kept him from being "too elated." It helped him to be more humble. What was this thorn in the flesh? Why did Paul ask for it to be removed? Why did Paul eventually become accepting of it and even see it as a "blessing in disguise"?

There is much scholarly debate concerning this "thorn in the flesh." Some have proposed that the thorn was "spiritual, for example, some particular temptation."[4] Others suggest that the thorn was that of persecution.[5] Still others conclude that Paul suffered from a physical ailment such as "epilepsy, migraine, a speech impediment, . . . or malarial fever."[6] A church member gave me another theory: poor eyesight. But whatever this thorn was, it was something that gave Paul considerable trouble and concern.

Paul did what most Christians do when faced with hardship or suffering: he prayed that God would remove it. Paul had no desire simply to suffer for the sake of suffering. So "three times" Paul asked God to remove this "thorn," but the thorn remained. Eventually, Paul accepted the "thorn" as something he would have to live with. His acceptance was initiated in part by God's response to his request.

In verse 9, we discover these words of God: "My grace is sufficient for you, for my power is made perfect in weakness." God did not say, "Grin and bear it." God did not command, "Endure patiently!" Rather, God suggested to Paul that in the midst of personal pain and aggravation, one has the possibility of becoming aware of divine presence and power.

We have no indication that Paul ever prayed again that the thorn be taken away. We are to assume that he lived with the reality of its nagging presence; we are left with many unanswered questions concerning this thorn. Yet in one sense it really does not matter what Paul's thorn was or whether it was a physical, mental, or spiritual ailment. What is important is that Paul resigned himself to living with the thorn and, even more, to believing it carried a blessing with it: humility.

Whenever I hear someone claim that God always gives us exactly what we pray for or that a Christian's life is one of prosperity and ease, I remember Paul's experience. Paul's prayer was answered, but it was not fulfilled.

Paul did not receive what he requested; he received what he most needed. God did not take away the thorn, or the pain, or the circumstance. Instead, God gave Paul the power to endure with hope and patience.

I believe God often relates to us in this way. God does not always spare us from pain, but God always gives us means of enduring and growing and maturing. One of Paul's assertions to the church at Corinth is that God will not allow us to be tested beyond our strength—our strength, that is, when coupled with the power of God (1 Cor. 10:13).

A favorite quote from my church's Bible study program is about someone who had obviously suffered from many "thorns." A woman who had suffered much in her life was talking informally with God: "Lord, I know you won't put on me more than I can bear, but I sure wish you didn't have so much confidence in me!"

> *Paul's prayer was answered, but it was not fulfilled.*

Paul would have agreed with the philosophy of this woman. Paul had suffered from many hardships, insults, persecutions, and calamities, but he finally had learned that they could be a sign of his weakness and, in turn, God's strength. This is why Paul could understand the thorn in his side not as a terrible curse but as a mysterious gift, a gift that kept him humble instead of dangerously overconfident.

Paul was a wise person. He recognized the thorns of his life, accepted them, even learned from them. What was Paul's "thorn in the flesh"? I personally lean toward the idea of a physical ailment of some sort—something that was nagging, aggravating, painful, but not totally debilitating. Since I have suffered from migraines, that would be my nomination for Paul's thorn. But whatever the affliction, the important thing to understand is that Paul simply learned to live with it, even seeing it as a strange kind of blessing.

So what does Paul's experience have to do with us? Quite a lot, I believe. We should readily identify with Paul's initial problem. An old spiritual might be revised to proclaim a truth: "All God's chill'ens got thorns!"

Everyone has a thorn—or two or three. Does anyone have a physical ailment, handicap, blemish, or disability? Does anyone live near someone who is a pain in the neck? I would call that something of a thorn, wouldn't you? Do you have an oppressive boss, a troublesome family member, a vicious enemy? Do you suffer from recurring pain? Chances are, you have a thorn in your flesh, a thorn in your side.

Most of us have learned how to deal with our thorns. Our favorite way of coping is to show our thorns to others. If we have something that causes us pain, we talk about it to a spouse or friend—or anyone who will listen!

When I play racquetball and get hit with the ball, I can't wait to show that horrible red blotch to my wife and say, "See my terrible bruise, Honey?" And she responds so compassionately, "Why do you like to play that game? You know you're going to get hit!" She still does not understand that I don't enjoy getting hit. I just enjoy showing my bruises if I get hit. I always want sympathy for my pain.

Many of us are like that. We don't like our thorns but we love to show our wounds. We like to complain and whimper. If we have a thorn in our side, then we want some real empathy! Many of us have shown our thorns, complained about our thorns so much that we have become a "thorn" to those about us. Like children seeking sympathy, we have shown our tiny splinters and large thorns to anyone who would look and listen. And we insist: "But my thorn really hurts!"

Perhaps some of us have even followed Paul's initial step; we have prayed for God to remove the thorns that plague us. We see no reason why we should have to bear our thorn forever. Someone should be able to pull out the thorn and make it stop hurting so much. Who can stand living a whole life with all that pain?

Like Paul, most of us have asked God to remove the thorns that bring us great pain. But only a few of us have been able to move on to Paul's second or third step. Few of us are willing to hear God's answer. The one God gave to Paul was: "You must learn to live with your thorn!"

Are you willing right now to live with all your existing

thorns? Can you resign yourself to the idea that you may *always* have such a condition, such a problem, such an ailment, such an enemy, such a cross to bear? Can you accept that a Christian is not exempted from suffering, not protected from thorns?

For many of us, grudging acceptance is about as gracious as we can muster. We may be able to tolerate those blasted thorns, but don't ask us to like them or welcome them. We never will stop looking at them, showing them to others, thinking about them, picking at them. We will endure them, but we will *never* stop protesting. We know they are not supposed to be there.

> *Can you accept that a Christian is not exempted from suffering, not protected from thorns?*

Paul was light years ahead of us. He was wise enough to understand that the thorn in his flesh kept him from a false security, an unhealthy arrogance, a cold complacency. Without the experience of thorns, how can one appreciate Christ's suffering? How can one be compassionate with those who have to bear so much pain all their lives? Thorns are not always a curse. Thorns can even bring families together, encourage humility, or remind us of blessings.

Lucky for us, some thorns are only temporary. Some thorns can be extracted and the pain subsides, the wound heals. Sometimes the sickness ends, the rebellious child matures, the enemy becomes a friend, the headaches stop, the boss retires, the cantankerous church member moves to the lake or transfers to another church, the facial complexion finally clears up.

All thorns are not forever, and we should be grateful for that. Some are extracted and our wounds are allowed to heal. But other thorns may be with us for a lifetime. Some of us will *always* be hard of hearing or have poor eyesight or suffer from arthritis. Some of us will have to live with our unwanted features, unwanted relatives, unwanted neighbors, unwanted hardships for the rest of our lives.

So we need to know what to do when the thorns won't go away—thorns that resist the needle, thorns that stay with us day after painful day. Do you have a thorn in mind, your very own thorn? Given your particular thorn, you have several choices. You can continue to show it to people. You can complain about it, whimper a lot or a little. You can become bitter or feel mistreated.

Or you can ask God to remove it, if you have not done so already. But if the thorn persists, you might follow the example of Paul. You might ask God to help you deal creatively with your thorn, especially if it is going to be with you for a while. Perhaps you need to ask God for strength to endure the pain, aggravation, or frustration.

Paul apparently stopped asking that the thorn be removed. He did not enjoy the pain, but carrying the thorn around was not without benefit.

If we are to bear patiently our thorns, we need some word from God to help us. Thorns can cause so much pain! They cannot easily be ignored. What "word" would help prevent infection, ward off self-pity and bitterness? God's answer to Paul surely is addressed to us as well. God said, "My grace is sufficient for you, for my power is made perfect in weakness."

God's grace is sufficient for you and me! God's grace is sufficient even if we carry these thorns always, even if we suffer. Even if we don't decide at this moment what to do with our thorns, when the sharp pain comes, we will have to decide. You see, you can't ignore a thorn.

> *"My grace is sufficient for you, for my power is made perfect in weakness."*

Remember our choices? We can complain or become bitter. We can feel sorry for ourselves or whimper. We can parade our thorns in front of everybody, begging for their deepest sympathy, while forgetting that they, too, carry thorns. We can endure the pain as a proud martyr: "Look at me. I'm so brave. I carry my thorns without shedding a tear. Now I'm better than everyone else." We can protest to God and the world that it is unfair; we suffer too much. Something must be done! Or we can remember an early missionary who suffered dearly. This man did not deserve to suffer, yet he carried a thorn wherever he went. We can remember this man as our splinters telegraph their messages of pain, as our thorns throb in our sides. We can remember this man and remember, too, the words of God that set him free: "My grace is sufficient for you."

That really is the bottom line. Is God's grace sufficient for you or not? Is God's grace sufficient even with the nagging thorns in your side, the aggravating splinters in your hands?

Just tell me, "Is God's grace sufficient?"

> *But with me it is a very small thing that I should be judged by you or by any human court. I do not even judge myself. It is the Lord who judges me.*
> *1 Corinthians 4:3, 4c*

Living with Critics!

*H*ave you ever received any criticism? Has negative criticism ever gotten under your skin? Have you spent too much of your life trying to please your critics? What would you really like to say to your greatest critic—maybe an overly critical parent, an aggressive spouse, a persistent boss, or a belligerent enemy?

My guess is that everyone has been criticized, not once but many, many times. I also am sure that we all have been hurt by criticism at some point in our life, perhaps even traumatized. But many of us also might reluctantly admit that we often have benefited from criticism.

Criticism is all around us. Let's face it; we are a nit-picking culture. Criticism is especially prevalent in sports and politics. There are two positions I never would want to hold: the quarterback of an NFL football team or the presidency of the United States. Both positions may offer some prestige and tons of money, but that hardly balances the harsh criticism that goes with the job. How would you like everyone in the country grading your work for your first one hundred days on the job? How would you handle the jeers of the crowd if your passes were off the mark—even after offering your body as a living sacrifice to three hundred-pound opposing linemen?

But whether we are Troy Aikman or President Clinton or just an average citizen, criticism will still come our way. Most of us would love to live without it but we are forced to live *with* it. Many years ago I had what I consider my hardest years of ministry. I forced myself to ignore an underground newspaper that criticized my ministry and the staff of the church. I also dealt with an avalanche of criticism—not so much about ministerial performance as about personality. During the early years of ministry, I was told that I did not smile enough, or I had failed to speak to someone as they passed by me in the hall on Sunday morning—even though I was talking to someone else at the time.

You can imagine how much such criticism helped me to smile and to be more relaxed! That period was not a particularly fun time in my ministry.

It was during that time that I discovered a book titled *How Can Everything Be All Right When Everything Is All Wrong?* by Lewis Smedes. The fourth chapter was of enormous help to me. It was actually a sermon based on a text from Paul, a text that was unfamiliar to me. The title of the chapter was "All the World's a Critic, and You're Tired of Getting the Reviews."

I thought to myself, "Now *that's* the chapter I need to read first!"

The chapter was filled with insights of how to handle criticism. It was based on Paul's message to his critics at Corinth. The text and Smedes's main points were very freeing to me. They lifted a weight off my shoulders and helped dissipate some of my suppressed anger. I was not totally free to disregard feedback, but it did help to put things in perspective. It softened the blows.

All of us will have to face criticism, if not now, then at

some point in our future. Some of the criticisms will be superficial, some profound, some warranted, some invalid. Some will be shared with us face-to-face as the scripture suggests. Some will be broadcast for everyone to hear.

> *All the world's a critic, and you're tired of getting the reviews.*

We who must learn to deal with criticism, especially the adverse kind, would do well to follow Paul's advice. Receive again his words. They offer a new freedom: "With me it is a very small thing that I should be judged by you or by any human court. I do not even judge myself. . . . It is the Lord who judges me" (1 Cor. 4:3-4).

In this text Paul shares with us three critics that we each must face—our neighbor, our innermost self, and our God. How well we handle these critics will reflect our level of maturity and our growth in the Christian life. Properly understood and kept in their rightful place, these critics can make our lives better and more meaningful. Given unrestricted power, these critical demands can shatter our lives or enslave us to false loyalties.

1. The first critic: the neighbor. Paul must have been personally and painfully aware of the dangers of criticism. But he was not willing to let criticisms from church members dominate his life. He writes to the church at Corinth, "With me it is a very small thing that I should be judged by you or by a human court." What do you think Paul was telling the Corinthians? Bug off? Cool it?

At the very least Paul was telling the Corinthians that he was not ready to follow their every whim or give in to their petty criticisms. In a polite way Paul was telling these disgruntled members that their criticisms might matter some, but not much. He was giving them notice that he was *God's* servant, not their *slave.*

They might measure his ministry by their standards and find him lacking, but such findings never would be conclusive or binding. God alone is our ruler. God alone gives us the ultimate measure of our worth.

Many of us would like to have the courage to follow Paul's approach. We would like to be able to say to our critics, especially the petty and caustic ones, "Your opinion does not really matter to me." We would like to be able to say, "My purpose in life is not to answer to your criticisms or to seek to please you. I have a higher calling."

> *If the criticism is unfair or untrue, we are twice wounded.*

Most of us would like to feel less vulnerable to the darts of criticism that people hurl at us, but when criticism does come, our armor is so easily pierced. (Oh, if only we had thicker skin!)

If the criticism is unfair or untrue, we are twice wounded. But if we let such criticism lead to hate or despair, we are twice defeated.

Most of us yearn for Paul's position—to be able to stand up to human criticism and declare: "I hear you. I will take what you said under advisement, but I will not blindly heed you or commit to serve you. I will not concentrate my efforts to appease anyone except my Creator." Such a statement of intent brings new freedom. It does not take away the sting of criticism. It does keep the critic's poison from being fatal.

In this passage Paul stresses our freedom from the tyranny of criticism, yet we must be careful not to declare criticism our enemy. Indeed, it can be our friend. Paul, for example, often used criticism to help the church improve. He wanted the church to hear and heed his message, not ignore his criticisms. Criticisms should *always* be heard. They should be sifted through very carefully to determine their truthfulness and then adjustments should be made if needed.

Untrue criticism hurts us and makes us angry. True criticism exposes us and makes us defensive. Criticism, whether true or untrue, is almost always painful.

But if we try to avoid pain by blocking out all criticism, we eliminate a primary way of learning the truth about ourselves. We forfeit a chance to grow. Even our enemies who criticize us may be doing us a favor by accident.

Antisthenes, a cynical philosopher, once wrote, "There are only two people who can tell you the truth about yourself—an enemy who has lost his temper, and a friend who loves you dearly."[7] A criticism, even if from an enemy, never should be dismissed without searching for its truth. Even so, Paul would remind us of an even greater danger: to choose to follow the demands of fellow critics, to become a slave to their values and judgments.

To follow such a course, a course of being manipulated by another person's judgment, is becoming a ventriloquist's helper—that's right, a dummy! Responding to a criticism should come only after first hearing it and discerning its truth. However, new directions in our lives should be to please God, not our loudest critics.

2. The second critic: the self. Paul's statement is, "I do not even judge myself." I do not believe that Paul was suggesting that we never evaluate ourselves or assess our behavior or motives. Paul exercised such self-evaluation on numerous occasions. Such self-scrutiny is one activity that separates us from other animals. We can transcend our own experience and judge it, evaluate it, call it good or bad, right or wrong. Paul is not asking us to ever abandon being our own critic. Rather, he is warning that such judgment is always inconclusive, just as the criticism from others is inconclusive.

There is good reason Paul put little stock in self-criticism or self-appraisal: it is rarely accurate. Few people have a realistic understanding of themselves. Many think more highly of themselves than they ought to think. Many think much less of themselves than they ought to think. Such self-judgment often is so strongly held that no amount of input from the outside can budge it.

I have met people (perhaps you have, also) who have a glaring fault or two, but they are totally blind to such deficiencies. I have met others whom I judge to be humble, loving, gentle people, but who see themselves as ordinary and somewhat unworthy.

Such cases give strength to Paul's notion that the self is no more reliable a critic than our neighbor. We may judge ourselves worthy; God may find us wanting. We may judge ourselves unworthy; God may declare us righteous.

3. The third critic: our Creator. This critic knows our every fault, our every flaw. This critic knows about the impure motives for our outwardly good deeds. This critic knows all of our tricks—rationalization, passing the buck, neutralizing our conscience, playing the martyr. This critic knows the creature.

Paul almost totally dismissed the criticisms of the Corinthian church. He also has questioned the accuracy of self-judgment. Paul concluded that there is only one valid critic for our lives, only one who can judge our worth: God, our Creator.

If we can pass God's test, if somehow we can receive God's acceptance, if God through mercy can call us good, then we are given a great new freedom.

Paul would neither have us ignore criticism from others nor suggest that we never take an honest look at ourselves. What Paul wants for us is a freedom he enjoyed, a freedom from being a slave to the whims and petty judgments of others, and from scurrying to and fro to make sure everyone likes us (an impossible task, by the way). Paul wants us to enjoy such freedom. But to do so we must begin where Paul begins—with God.

We must make our aim in life to please not our mother, father, boss, the company, spouse, friends, or even ourselves. We must make our ultimate aim to please God. We must be willing to accept God's judgment upon our lives and realize that we often fall short of who God calls us to be. Finally, we must draw into our inner being our Great Critic's words of grace: "You are forgiven!"

Once we can truly accept both God's judgment and God's grace, we have a new freedom over criticism. The poisoned darts still will fly. They will sting, but they will not kill or enslave us. As long as we serve God and not the whims of others, a special freedom is ours.

> *As long as we serve God and not the whims of others, a special freedom is ours.*

This new freedom is not a freedom to ignore criticism. It is freedom from slavery to our critics. Paul achieved such a freedom and proclaimed it to the church at Corinth. He did so to invite them into a new liberty, a liberty available even to us.

Are we ready to speak to our critics a word they do not want to hear, the same words that Paul spoke to the church at Corinth?

"With me it is a very small thing that I should be judged by you or by any human court. I do not even judge myself. . . . It is the Lord who judges me (1 Cor. 4:3-4). God is our critic, our judge. But God is also our redeemer. We can dare to read our reviews now. God has judged us and then declared us righteous by grace! We are free from our critics' snare. Thanks be to God! Amen.

> *Do not be overcome by evil, but overcome evil with good. Romans 12:21*

Overcoming Evil!

H ow many of you have ever overcome evil? How many have returned evil for evil? How many times have the hateful actions of others led you to anger? How often have you plotted revenge? How often have you actually got that revenge?

Every one of us has had evil done to us. Some of us have suffered from childhood abuse, some from destructive relationships, some from social injustice, some from betrayal, some from lies or false rumors. Some of us have been victimized by enemies who meant us harm. Some of us have suffered simply because of the negligence of another.

Bottom line? We all have been victims of human evil. Some of us have had more than our fair share. Some of us have had only a taste. And some of us have been relatively lucky. But all of us have been victimized by evil—by the harmful actions of others. All of us have had to decide *many* times in our lives, "Will I retaliate? Should I return evil for evil?" All of us also have had the possibility of overcoming evil with good!

Paul, in his letter to the church at Rome, echoes the message of Jesus. It was Jesus who asked us to "love [our] enemies" (Matt. 5:44) and to "pray for those who abuse

[us]" (Luke 6:28). It was Jesus who told us we would be blessed if people reviled and persecuted us and uttered all kinds of evil against us for his sake (Matt. 5:11). But, of course, that kind of experience does not feel very blessed at the time, does it? Jesus suggests, in fact, that our reward will be "in heaven" and not necessarily in this life.

Paul's words are very similar to the words of Jesus. Paul says, "Bless those who persecute you. . . ." He also tells us never to repay evil for evil. Instead, we are to minister to our enemy—to provide needed food or drink.

Paul is addressing us, both as individuals and as a community of faith. How can we stop the rampage of evil actions in our society, and how do we prevent ourselves from becoming double victims of evil—hurt first by the deed and then paralyzed by resentment or hate? Paul has one answer for both the community and the individual: love! Only love can defeat evil.

I share with you three levels of response to evil done against us.

First, remember some evil done against you. Has someone ever harmed you, hurt you? Do you still harbor some ill feeling? Perhaps Paul's advice is especially for you. The first level of response when people do evil to us, whether intentionally or accidentally, is this: to decide not to retaliate. It is human nature to respond in kind. If someone hurts us, there is a strong urge to hurt them in return or to wish them harm.

The first Christian response called for is to refrain from striking back. Turning the other cheek won't work if we already have returned the blow.

Avoiding retaliation is the first step in preventing escalation. If we do not strike back, there is a chance that the abuse will stop, but, of course, there is no guarantee. This first step is the battle over the body. If we are attacked physically, we are not to attack back with our bodies. If we are attacked by words, we are not to attack back with words.

I am not suggesting that there is no place for self-defense. But true self-defense is not intended to bring harm to others—only to prevent further harm to self. That is why the first rule of self-defense is to run or cry for help.

Paul asks that we repay no one evil for evil, that we try to break the vicious cycle of "evil for evil" that creates ill will and endless violence. He suggests that we not seek revenge or retaliation.

The second battle is that of the mind and heart. Many Christians win the first battle; many Christians take the first step by refusing to return evil for evil but fail miserably in the second battle. Many Christians do not harm the enemy; they do not retaliate. But they later bring harm to themselves by harboring ill feeling or hatred. Booker Washington reveals the foolishness of such a stance when he says, "I will not allow any man to make me lower myself by hating him."[8]

Too many Christians pat themselves on the back for not retaliating and then bury the evil inside themselves. They have transformed the hurt into hatred and thus doubled their injury. But when actions against us are allowed to become hatred, we are thus overcome by evil. When this happens, evil is not curtailed but rather multiplied!

This brings us now to the most difficult response to evil actions against us. Paul asks us to do more than to refrain from retaliation, more than to beat down the feelings of ill will and anger. He asks that we actively seek to bless our enemy. Jesus tells us to "love our enemies." Paul says in Romans that we are to feed them if they are hungry, give them drink if they are thirsty. Paul also asks that we "bless them."

What is requested begins with the inner self. We are to bless with our minds and hearts: and to wish our enemies well.

We then are to bless them with our actions, doing acts of kindness for them.

> *We are to bless with our minds and hearts: and to wish our enemies well.*

Surely we are now on the level of sainthood! It is one thing to refrain from striking back. It is one thing not to harbor hatred for harm done to us. But it is something rather extraordinary to actually offer a loving gesture to our enemies! Maybe these are acts reserved only for people like Jesus and Paul!

Several months ago I discovered diggings and scratch marks all over the ground in our backyard after hand seeding the entire yard with fescue. It was looking very good, totally covered—at least *before* this strange invasion. After careful investigation, my best guess was an armadillo or possum, so I went to our city's Animal Control Department for a trap. Before I caught the little critter (which happened to be a possum), it had destroyed much of the grass in the backyard and had broken the lattice work around our deck. The critter evidently needed a secure home under our wooden deck.

After I caught the possum, I called animal control to see what I should do. "Put the trap out front but in the shade. We don't want the possum to get hot before we pick him up," they said. After this darling had torn up our yard and underpinning, do you think I cared if he got hot? I thought I showed great restraint just by allowing it to live!

But if I have trouble forgiving possums—God's creatures that wish neither me nor my yard any harm—just think how hard it will be to forgive people who work against me. Difficult it may be, but that is clearly *my* calling, and *yours!*

This is the level of Christian behavior that holds the promise of changing lives, not just our lives, but the lives of those who bring us harm. Whether our act is offering food, kindness, or forgiveness, there is immense power in the victim's showing love and mercy to the offender. It is a power that may well convict and convert!

Some may remember with great excitement one verse of our text. It was the verse that talked about our kindnesses heaping hot coals on the heads of our enemies. Did you enjoy those words? "No, 'if your enemies are hungry, feed them; if they are thirsty, give them something to drink; for by doing this you will heap burning coals on their heads'" (Rom. 12:20). Nice image, don't you think? Did you know that sometimes it does not help the minister to read the commentaries. Sometimes it would be better if we did not consult the biblical scholars. They don't always tell us what we want to hear. None of them I read said if we treat our enemies nicely that God will see to it that they will be sufficiently punished, and that the nicer we treat them the more fiery punishment they will get. Rather, the commentaries suggested that the "burning coals" were not a reference to eternal punishment but rather inner remorse.[9] Kindness to the enemy would likely produce a sense of guilt or repentance. No true revenge here!

From time to time I have seen kindness produce remorse. But I also have seen it fail. But even without a guarantee it is worth a try. Why? Because not only do *we* stand to gain, but also the person we befriend may gain. We, by our act of kindness, may rid ourselves of hard feelings and at the same time give the enemy a chance to realize wrongdoing. Sometimes that change can be life-giving!

So how are you with your enemies right now? Do you have peace of mind? Do you have that great freedom that comes with having no hard feelings? Or are you burdened with a resentment that is choking your inner spirit?

Do you want to shoot the person, or lock him or her up in a cage? Would you be so thoughtful as to keep the cage out of the sun or would you enjoy letting them sweat a little? What kind of coals would you select for their heads: the real flesh-burning kind or the coals of remorse and repentance?

Some of us might be tempted to accuse Paul of being quite unrealistic. How could he believe it possible to bless one's enemies? What made him think that we ever could follow in Jesus' footsteps and forgive people who harm us and pray for those who persecute us? Jesus lived what he taught; we know that. Even on the cross Jesus petitioned God on behalf of those who mocked him, those who perse-cuted him. Do you remember Jesus' words? "Father, forgive them; for they do not know what they are doing" (Luke 23:34). But for us to follow Jesus' example? Get serious!

Surely Paul knew of Jesus' words about loving our ene-mies. But I do not think that is the only reason Paul came to believe those words. I think Paul may have first believed those words when he heard them echoed by the first Chris-tian martyr, Stephen, just before he was stoned to death. I believe Paul's evil actions might well have been overcome by the saintly actions of Stephen. In the book of Acts we discover the story:

> When they heard . . . [Stephen's preaching, they] ground their teeth at Stephen. But filled with the Holy Spirit, he gazed into heaven and saw the glory of God and Jesus standing at the right hand of God. "Look," he said, "I see the heavens opened and the Son of Man standing at the right hand of God!" But they covered their ears, and with a loud shout all rushed together against him. Then they dragged him out of the city and began to stone him; and the witnesses laid their coats at the feet of a young man named Saul. While they were stoning Stephen, he prayed,

"Lord Jesus, receive my spirit." Then he knelt down and cried out in a loud voice, "Lord, do not hold this sin against them." When he had said this, he died. And Saul approved of their killing him. (Acts 7:54-60; 8:1*a*)

"And Saul (later to be called Paul) approved of their killing him." I believe Paul never forgot the words that Stephen spoke to him and to the crowd: "Lord, do not hold this sin against them."

Those words must have been like burning coals on Paul's head. Those words well may have made Paul open to the Christian faith. An evil act by religious people was met, not with curses or anger or hatred, but with the soft words of forgiveness and mercy. Paul's evil may well have been overcome by Stephen's magnanimous act of mercy.

> *"Lord, do not hold this sin against them."*

There is so much evil in our world today. All of us will experience hateful and harmful actions or vicious words from people. Such actions will cry out for retaliation. But as Christians we are called to a different level of response. We should not respond as spoiled or self-righteous people or simply react in the fury of the moment. Rather, we should respond to evil done to us empowered by our loving Creator—empowered to do good, empowered to forgive even as God forgives us!

Paul speaks the truth from the example of Jesus, but perhaps also from his own experience. He was forgiven by Stephen. Now Paul stands ready to forgive others. So we may trust his words: they have been tested by fire, by burning coals on his head.

> *Do not be overcome by evil, but overcome evil with good.*

Bless those who persecute you; bless and do not curse them. Rejoice with those who rejoice, weep with those who weep. Live in harmony with one another; do not be haughty, but associate with the lowly; do not claim to be wiser than you are. Do not repay anyone evil for evil, but take thought for what is noble in the sight of all. If it is possible, so far as it depends on you, live peaceably with all. Beloved, never avenge yourselves, but leave room for the wrath of God; for it is written, "Vengeance is mine, I will repay, says the Lord." No, "if your enemies are hungry, feed them; if they are thirsty, give them something to drink; for by so doing this you will heap burning coals on their heads." Do not be overcome by evil, but overcome evil with good.

(Rom. 12:14-21)

> *Finally, beloved, whatever is true, whatever is honorable, whatever is just, whatever is pure, whatever is pleasing, whatever is commendable, if there is any excellence and if there is anything worthy of praise, think about these things.*
> *Philippians 4:8*

Beyond Positive Thinking

Would our lives be any different if we decided to take the *National Enquirer*'s approach to life instead of heeding Paul's advice to the church at Philippi? Paul tells us that we are to contemplate the true, honorable, just, pure, lovely, and gracious.

> *Paul tells us that we are to contemplate the true, honorable, just, pure, lovely, and gracious.*

Would we be any different if we chose instead to think on the scandalous, the racy, the perverted, the bizarre, the ugly, the caustic, the sensational? Both of these alternatives have an appeal. One offers excitement and piques our curiosity. One speaks a message of hope and wholeness and peace.

I trust that you will not be surprised if I choose to argue in favor of Paul's advice. Paul is not proposing that Christians shut their eyes to the problems of the society. Rather, he suggests that Christians, in the midst of a troubled world, must be able to see the signs of the kingdom, the signs of God, which are literally all around. Does anyone here deny that such good things exist? Does not Christian truth occasionally wave its banner before us? Does it not proclaim its message: "Hate is wrong, honesty is smart, intimacy is better than shallow relationships"?

And what of honor? Do you remember Jessica, the young girl who fell into a hole that quickly caved in on her and kept her captive for hours? Remember how the rescuers refused to be seen as heroes and instead pointed to the indomitable spirit of this tiny, happy child? It was a touching story devoid of self-praise. It was something honorable.

Have we not all seen purity? What can be more pure than the peaceful countenance of a sleeping infant? And our candidates for loveliness could go on and on: the soft pink kiss of a sunset, the emotional embrace of violins, the rustic charm of the desert, the penetrating smile of caring eyes, the words of comfort from a friend. Few would argue that things of beauty and honor do not exist today, but they are not always a vivid part of our everyday consciousness. Paul would change all that. He urges us to: *"Think on these things!"*

Paul, I believe, would readily agree that the person and Spirit of Christ also reveal such qualities. Christ spoke the truth. His life was pure, his actions just, gracious, and lovely. Remember Jesus sitting in the midst of the children? Does the image of justice come to life as we picture Christ driving out the moneychangers? Do you see graciousness and humility in Jesus' act of washing the feet of his disciples?   Our problem with following Paul's advice is not the absence of the qualities that Paul alludes to; they are present in our world just as they were in Paul's day. One does not have to resort to wishful thinking or fantasy. Such things as truth, graciousness, goodness, beauty exist in our day, in our city, within the perimeters of our vision.

Our first step, however, is not really to *think* on these things. Our first step, strangely enough, is simply to *see* these things. Search the daily newspaper for the pure, the just, the honorable, the good, the inspiring, the lovely. Were it not for an occasional human interest story rationed out to us, I'm not sure one could find many of Paul's qualities on the front page of the daily newspaper. We may have to look elsewhere. *Seeing* the qualities of God may be our best strategy for contemplating these qualities that Paul holds before us!

During my ministry I have met several people who have been able to live out Paul's words in the midst of tragedy, uncertainty, and ugliness. Through faith, divine presence, and personal courage, one lady in particular comes to mind who has been able to think of the lovely, the good, the positive, the hopeful, and the gracious. She has not denied the negative; she has simply relegated it to a place of limited prominence—in the back of her mind. Her thoughts, she says, must be on the positive. Her energies must be directed toward the good she can do for her critically ill daughter. She must not be paralyzed by visions of the past or fears of the future. After witnessing her life, I now can believe even more the words of Paul. I know one particular person who is living out those inspiring words of Philippians 4.

How is your vision lately? Are you farsighted—capable of seeing the problems of the future, the possible pitfalls, the eventual hardships—but unable to see the beauty right under your nose? Are you nearsighted and only able to see clearly the problems and ugliness of the immediate surrounding, but unable to see the signs of hope, joy, and peace in the distance?

71

Are you unable to think on the things of God because you are unable to bring them into focus as you live day by day?

> *Are you nearsighted and only able to see clearly the problems and ugliness of the immediate surrounding, but unable to see the signs of hope, joy, and peace in the distance?*

It takes special vision to see the good and the lovely in the midst of the bad and the ugly. It is sometimes difficult to discern the just and the pure in our present world, but they all are there. Sometimes it is a matter of taking time to look. But mostly it is a matter of deciding what it is we *want to see.*

If you want to find ugliness in your spouse, you will find it—or it will find you. If you decide life is bad or tragic or a bummer, your head will spin from the sights you can see—sights of injustice, cruelty, perversion, and ugliness. In movies like *Schindler's List* we can see only the atrocities and ignore the acts of compassion, the changes of heart. Or we can learn to look beneath the surface for qualities that Paul has urged us to find. We then can see a Gentile exchange his prejudice for empathy, his self-centeredness for self-giving.

Paul is not calling us to shut our eyes to ugliness and contemplate in a vacuum "sugar plum visions" of how things might be. He is hoping we will be able to see the beauty in the midst of ugliness, the joy on the fringers of tragedy, the goodness intermingled with injustice and wrong.

It is easy to see beauty when there is nothing to obstruct the view. But Paul wants us to have images so vivid in our minds that they always will be a source of strength, a reminder that these, too, are a part of our world. We should never forget the image of sunshine in the midst of a storm or the beauty of the dawn during our darkest hour.

> *He is hoping we will be able to see the beauty in the midst of ugliness, the joy on the fringes of tragedy, the goodness intermingled with injustice and wrong.*

Jesus had the vision Paul wishes for us. Jesus asked that we consider the lilies. He did not tell us to ponder the weeds. Jesus was never overwhelmed by ugliness. He did not recoil from the leper or the thief or the beggar. In disfigured or distraught people, Jesus saw the real beauty that others failed to see. Jesus saw not a thief on the cross, but a man worthy of paradise; not a short, unscrupulous scoundrel in a tree, but one capable of generosity and service; not an adulterous woman, but a child of God ready to repent and be made whole.

If we are to be able to think the things of God, we must learn to see them through eyes of faith. We must learn to celebrate them, to make them a part of our vision.

Dr. Richard Selzer, a surgeon, had operated on a young woman and in order to remove a tumor, had had to cut a facial nerve. The operation had left one side of her mouth without muscle support. It drooped as though she suffered from palsy. "Will my mouth always be like this?" she asks. "Yes," I say, "it will. It is because the nerve was cut." She nods and is silent. But the young [husband] smiled. "I like it," he says. "It is kind of cute." Unmindful, he bends to kiss her crooked mouth, and I am so close I see how he

twists his own lips to accommodate hers to show her that
their kiss still works[10]

> *If we are to be able to think the things of God, we
> must learn to see them through eyes of faith.*

Do you have eyes that see truth, beauty, goodness, hope,
and joy? Can you see these gifts of God even in the midst
of ugliness, even when the light is dim and darkness is
heavy? If you can see even then, you will receive extra
meaning from Paul's words.

Paul says, whatever is true, whatever is lovely, whatever is
of good report—we are to *think* on these things. We are to
ponder them, remember them, see them, meditate on
them.

You say you are too busy—too busy to think about these
things. You don't want to be unrealistic. You are not good
at daydreaming. If you don't have time to think about
these things, how do you have time to worry? If you don't
have time to think about good things, hopeful things,
beautiful things, why is your mind often filled with fears
and anxieties and ugly thoughts? Are fears and worries
and ugliness closer to the truth, closer to reality? You say
you don't have time to meditate or pray or think positive
thoughts. Weren't you in the recliner the other day? Or
were you watching television? And what was the message of
that show? Was it helpful to your living? Did you find time
to read that horrible account in the newspaper? You say
you don't have time to think about positive things. If you
ask many who were prisoners of war, they will tell you that
what kept them alive was not "having a realistic understanding of the seriousness of their situation." What kept

many of them alive was the contemplation of God or of a loved one. These meditations were real even though they were not so evident in that situation. Love and truth still existed. In the midst of the horrors of war, the things of God were not easy to see. But to see them meant Life!

Paul urged the Christians at Philippi to be diligent in their focus on God. To worship God is to give thanks for the gifts of God, to give thanks for the signs of God's presence and power in our world.

My friends, you have many choices in life, choices that will drastically shape your future. First of all, what will you choose to see as you look at life day by day? Will you mainly see disorder and tragedy? Will you fail to recognize goodness? Will you fill your mind with negative images, negative thoughts, or a negative outlook? Or will you see the healing, the therapy, that comes from love, beauty, and graciousness? Paul's advice is more than helpful. It does not separate the very happy from the fairly happy. How we *see* life and what we choose to *ponder* may prove to be the difference between joy and sorrow, hope and despair, and even life and death.

Beauty, love, hope, and goodness are in the world. You may find them in the strangest of places: on the bed of the terminally ill, in the face of a troubled child, in the midst of human suffering, or at the very heart of our laughter.

First, we must be able to see these things of God. We must affirm them and celebrate them. Then we are ready to follow Paul's advice:

Finally, beloved, whatever is true, whatever is honorable, whatever is just, whatever is pure, whatever is pleasing, whatever is commendable, if there is any excellence and if there is anything worthy of praise, think about these things.
(Phil. 4:8)

> *And not only that, but we also boast in our sufferings, knowing that suffering produces endurance, and endurance produces character, and character produces hope, and hope does not disappoint us, because God's love has been poured into our hearts through the Holy Spirit that has been given to us.*
> *Romans 5:3-5*

Hanging On!

his is the first in a series of sermons titled "Beyond Survival." The three sermons in the series are titled "Hanging On!" "Getting It Together!" and "Letting Go!" The basic premise of the series is that a Christian should expect many different stages in life—times of crises, times of taking stock, and times of blossoming. Each of these stages or seasons requires a different response.

> *Sometimes the best we can do is simply survive.*

Sometimes the best we can do is simply survive, to "hang in there." Sometimes we will be able to move beyond survival and begin the process of getting it all together, of plotting new and valid directions. Other times we will be able to discover a new dimension of living where we can bask in joy and inner peace. God's ultimate intention is not that we merely survive life, or that we merely *endure it.* God wants us to experience life in all its richness and goodness. God wants us to have life and have it abundantly!

I begin with the heaviest topic of the three sermons by exploring those times when endurance is required, when courage and patience are the order of the day. Have you ever experienced any of these times?

Picture in your mind the various images for the phrase, "hanging in there!" Do you have an image yet? Do you see a cat upside down, hanging by its claws from the ceiling? Do you imagine a person dangling from a cliff, saved only by a scrawny branch embedded in the rocks? Do you see someone with a panicked look, holding onto a rope for dear life? Whatever your image, the feeling is somewhere between desperation and quiet hope. Sometimes all we seem to be able to do is survive—to try hard just to keep our sanity; to face illness and pain with a determined grimace; to try one day at a time to deal with the terrible void that death has brought; to try to recover from the sting of a divorce; to endure the pain of having to watch someone we love fruitlessly live out their lives; to wrestle daily with the demons of our own desires and find our resistance weakening; to face the fact that there are no good alternatives to our present situation.

All of us want living to be more than merely existing, but aren't there times when that is about all we can muster? Sometimes all we are able to do is just hang on— to wait for the bugle call of the "cavalry," wait for some change in the world or in us!

Hanging on is a stance we may take even when our backs are not up against a wall. Sometimes we need to hang in there when things are just tough, when things are not going the way we would like.

Perhaps we have to endure a temporary illness. Or maybe we are trying to meet a deadline or survive an especially stressful week.

Sometimes we have to endure uncertain times of unemployment or of wondering if our house will ever sell. Endurance may be a common stance in our lives. There are times when we just have to keep "hanging on" until things are better. A layman of a church had an unusual but fitting expression. It was a takeoff on a familiar quote. His saying? "All's well that ends!" Life often requires of us some discipline, some willingness to persist, to keep trying. Life asks us to hang in there!

A pastor tells the story of his experience with Little League baseball as a child. In one game he was given the chance of becoming the hero or the klutz. It was his time at bat—two outs, two on base, and two runs behind. As he walked to the batter's box he looked up in the stands and saw, for the first time in his baseball career, the silhouette of his father.

Not only was the team watching, the fans watching, and the pitcher staring him down; but also his father's gaze was burning into the back of his uniform.

The young boy stood as tall as he could, with as much confidence as he could fake, as eager as a young brave embarking on his first hunt. On the first pitch he took his best cut. Strike one. He did not dare look back at the stands. He mustered all his strength again. The pitcher was glaring at him. The next pitch came like a bolt of lightning, but his second swing also rippled the air like thunder. Strike two.

The moment had come. What was it going to be—a hit or strike thee, the thrill of victory or the agony of defeat? Once more the pitcher hurled the white globe through the galaxies. Soon history would be made. He remembered that one goes around only once in life so he grabbed for all the gusto he could find and whirled his Louisville Slugger so fast it would have humbled the Babe. Strike three!

As he left the batter's box, half in tears, half in self-anger, the downcast boy looked through blurry eyes at the stands. His father was not there. But as he walked to the dugout his father stood before him, slapped him on the back and said, "My son, that is some swing you have! When you DO hit that ball it will be a homer! Just keep on swinging!"[11] So also the word comes to us in our time of testing: just keep on swinging, just keep on trying, just keep on hanging in there. Things will get better. Hang on!

As Christians our task begins with doing our part—by enduring, by trying, by doing our best to survive, and doing our best to improve. But such is the case for all people. All of us are expected to hang on and keep trying. What separates Christians from non-Christians is that Christians do not depend only on individual courage or determination. Most people are willing to keep trying for a while, to hang in there.

> *A Christian is called upon to be as optimistic as Jacob, who, after wrestling until dawn with an angel, was bold enough to ask for a blessing.*

But a Christian is called to do more than simply hang on. A Christian is urged to hang on with hope—to believe that there is a power beyond human power, a source of strength beyond inner strength. A Christian is called upon to be as optimistic as Jacob, who, after wrestling until dawn with an angel, was bold enough to ask for a blessing.

A Christian has the almost absurd notion that there is meaning even in suffering, that there is a blessing in every hardship, that there are things to be learned from pain, that hanging on always has some reward.

In his letter to the Corinthians, Paul acknowledges both the challenge and the benefits of the apostolic ministry. He writes:

> We are treated as impostors, and yet are true; as unknown, and yet are well known; as dying, and see—we are alive; as punished, and yet not killed; as sorrowful, yet always rejoicing; as poor, yet making many rich; as having nothing, and yet possessing everything. (2 Cor. 6:8*b*-10)

A Christian has the almost absurd notion that there is meaning even in suffering, that there is a blessing in every hardship, that there are things to be learned from pain, that hanging on always has some reward.

Christians believe that we should always have something for pain—not aspirin but something much more effective—God's presence and power! We are confident that no suffering is devoid of a blessing!

Maybe a tragedy brings a family closer together, or maybe it makes one more compassionate toward another's pain. Maybe an illness puts our everyday priorities in proper perspective. Maybe a failure brings much needed humility to our souls. Maybe we learn courage from dealing with constant pain. Maybe we learn to trust in God more than ourselves.

Suffering, pain, and hardship are not the enemies of the

Christian. They may not be planned or initiated by God, but they always can be used by God for some good.

When we hang on with hope, when we decide not to be content with survival, when we understand that pain may be as much a friend as it is an enemy, we are well on our way to growth in life and faith.

We all can be assured that we will experience some times of survival, times when we must do our best to hang in and hang on. Those times are not expected to be all happiness. But neither are they times to mope or give up in despair.

These trying times call us to believe in a God who suffers with us, who offers his strength, who is willing and able to find, somewhere amid the ugliness, tears, and pain, a flower, a hope, a rainbow, a shaft of light.

God wants more than survival for us. God wants endurance with a purpose and perseverance with a blessing. God wants us to hang on with hope.

Paul's word to the church at Rome goes beyond our normal way of thinking. Paul expects more from the church than simple endurance. He wants us to believe that in every circumstance we may find growth, or meaning, or even joy. He is daring enough to ask us to be grateful, in the midst of struggling, to be able to keep our heads above water!

Will you receive Paul's words? They are words beyond survival, words that do not stop with endurance but rush on to the fitting conclusion:

And not only that, but we also boast in our sufferings, knowing that suffering produces endurance, and endurance produces character, and character produces hope, and hope does not disappoint us, because God's love has been poured into our hearts through the Holy Spirit that has been given to us. (Rom. 5:3-5)

81

So what shall we say when life gets tough or when the darkness closes in? We say to ourselves and those about us: Keep on swinging! Keep on hoping! Hang on! There is a blessing somewhere!

> *And not only that, but we also boast in our sufferings, knowing that suffering produces endurance, and endurance produces character, and character produces hope, and hope does not disappoint us, because God's love has been poured into our hearts through the Holy Spirit that has been given to us.*
> *Romans 5:3-5*

> *Then Jesus asked him, "What is your name?"*
> *He replied, "My name is Legion; for we are*
> *many." Mark 5:9*

Getting It Together!

This series on "Beyond Survival" began with a word of encouragement to "hang in there!" We were encouraged to hang in there when things get tough, to believe that there is strength beyond our own inner resources. We were asked to hang on with hope. The images of hanging on were of a man dangling off a cliff, a cat hanging by its claws, or a panicked person dangling from a rope. Now we consider another phase of the Christian life: the time of "getting it together." The images change to the man at the top of the cliff, no longer ready to fall; the cat perched in a tree; and the person dangling from the rope, now on solid ground, thanks to the help of friends.

The question we now can raise is, "What are we to do when we have made it through the toughest part of the crisis, when we begin to realize that we will keep our sanity, that a normal existence is possible, that there is hope for moving ahead?" What are we going to do beyond survival? How will we get our bearings, and what will help make sense of it all?

Getting it together is an important exercise for every person. It is not done once and for all but many, many times during one's lifetime. Getting it together might include taking stock of ourselves, searching for a center for our lives, and finding a proper direction. It is a movement away from survival toward meaning; away from mere existence toward a full life. Getting it together is a time for focusing and gaining one's balance.

The Gospel reading is about a man who gets it all together—except in this case the initial work is done for him. Jesus frees him from an evil spirit. Jesus saves the man from his haunted existence and presents him the possibility of new life.

Legion has been so unlucky until now. He has been tortured by self and by society. But Legion's "luck" is about to change. Jesus wastes no time. Legion is put together instantly. There is no struggle, no process. The word from the Master brings immediate wholeness. Legion is no longer many; he is one! Legion now has it all together.

> *The word from the Master brings immediate wholeness. Legion is no longer many; he is one! Legion now has it all together.*

Most of us would like that kind of deliverance. We long for that kind of miraculous transformation. Not only would we like someone to save us from our crises and from our struggles to survive, but also to put us back together, to heal the divisions within us, and to still the demons that torture us. We want our lives to have the same happy ending that Legion had. We want to join Legion in being clothed in our right mind.

My hunch is that every Christian will not experience Legion's miracle in that same dramatic way. But every person has the opportunity for the same end result. Everyone can become whole and have peace of mind.

During my ministry I have seen countless Legions find wholeness. I have seen many people "get it together." But in most cases it took a while. Often the process required individual discipline and commitment. In most cases it took the help of friends. In all cases it involved the love and power of God!

When we are finally crawling out of our fight for survival, we want things to be instantly better. We want transformation and we want it now. We have fought so hard and for so long that we think we deserve a rest. But getting it together rarely happens overnight!

> *We have fought so hard and for so long that we think we deserve a rest. But getting it together rarely happens overnight!*

After suffering through a painful divorce, God does not simply zap us with instant self-esteem. After experiencing the loss of a spouse, one does not instantly adjust to such a different life. After succumbing to bad moral choices and behavior, one does not easily begin to win the battle over temptation. After having a close brush with death, one may quickly disregard old priorities, but new priorities take longer to establish.

Legion was fortunate to have such a radical and complete transformation. Jesus was there to assure him that he could "get it together." Such help is still available today. There are victory stories all around. Jesus' word and touch still have great power. Conversions, transformations, rebirths still take place. People who have hit rock bottom can discover the height and depth of God. People who face serious illness can take the time to reprioritize their lives. Those who have given way to their passions can discover a new moral goodness.

But one common strand seems to run through the experiences of the many people I've known who have battled for survival and finally have gotten it together: they have a clear understanding that they did not achieve health solely by their own power. They did not simply save themselves. They did not lift themselves by their own bootstraps.

Even though much self-discipline was required, they had to rely even more on the power of God and the support of others. Make no mistake about it: "getting it together" is a team sport!

But though God's power is essential and the support of friends is necessary, the role we play in getting it together is crucial as well.

To "get it together," our first step may be to take stock of ourselves. Or perhaps our first act should be confession, admitting that we have not been the person we should be. Or maybe our movement toward wholeness should begin with an abandonment of old priorities—priorities of business or success or some idealized picture of who we are supposed to be.

> *Make no mistake about it: "getting it together" is a team sport!*

To "get it together," we sometimes have to take the first step. Like Legion, we must cry out for help. We must admit our need. We must be willing to leave the comfort of nursing our grief, or the pleasure of sensuality, or the false security of possessions. We must believe that there is something more than mere existence, something more than being bound by chains of our old self. We must hope that there is possibility for love and hope and inner peace.

But maybe I'm the only one who has seen transformation. Maybe no one else has ever witnessed someone move from beyond survival to a full and rich life. Has anyone else ever seen a Legion "get it together"? Have you ever run across some old discarded chains? Have you, like Legion, experienced the terror of being "many," of being pulled apart? Have you experienced a process where it finally came together?

Throughout my ministry I have seen people move beyond survival. I have witnessed people lose a spouse but finally get it together. I have watched people battle addiction of all kinds and finally "get it all together." I have seen people change priorities and find a whole new dimension of life. I have witnessed people whose lives were fragmented find wholeness and peace of mind. I wholeheartedly believe in the possibility of "getting it together." I have seen it so many, many times.

Legion took an important first step. He stepped toward Jesus. He approached the One who knew about wholeness and abundance, about love and inner peace. And, most important, Legion knew he had a problem. He knew he was being pulled apart by the forces within. He wanted wholeness.

Getting it together often starts when we take a look at ourselves. We should expect such a look, if it is an honest appraisal, to be painful. We won't like everything we see. But to get it together we must know who we are.

Getting it together is not merely an exercise in self-scrutiny. It is a process that must acknowledge that we have a creative purpose and a Creator. How can we ever expect to have it all together if we are estranged from our Creator and from our fellow creatures? How can we be in sync with ourselves if we are not in sync with God? How can we expect to have our lives in order if we are out of relationship with the One who created order itself?

Our second text gives us further help in our journey toward wholeness. If we are going to "get it together" and keep it together, we will need more than an honest look at ourselves. We will need some direction; we will need a focus. We will need principles and values.

In Matthew's Gospel we discover a lawyer who asks Jesus an important question. He asks him, "Which commandment in the law is the greatest?" Jesus answered him with these words:

> "You shall love the Lord your God with all your heart, and with all your soul, and with all your mind." This is the greatest and first commandment. And a second is like it: "You shall love your neighbor as yourself." On these two commandments hang all the law and the prophets.   (Matt. 22:37*b*-40)

Want to "get it all together"? I would suggest that you not forget these words of Jesus. If we could "get it together" without love—and I don't think we can—I am certain that we could not keep it together without love.

The pieces won't really start fitting together until we look beyond ourselves to the needs of others.

Getting it together may well be a difficult task, even a complex task. A little self-scrutiny wouldn't be bad. Some honest reassessment also would be in order. Some genuine soul searching might be helpful. The pieces won't really start fitting together until we look beyond ourselves to the needs of others, until we nurture our grounding in God, until we realize that the principles of love are meant to bless others and to keep our lives full and rich.

Do any of you not have it together? Are people constantly telling you to grow up? Is your spiritual age a fraction of the age of your body? Are you exiting the survival stage and anxious to "put it all together"?

If your name is Legion, you may be in for a radical and immediate transformation. If you are like the rest of us, it may take some time and effort. But it is a struggle that is not to be focused primarily on the self. If it is, it will fail. To get it together, we must love God and love others. To discover *who* we are, we must finally realize *whose* we are.

> *I am the good shepherd. I know my own and my own know me. John 10:14*

Letting Go!

We have been exploring how our lives might be more than survival, more than mere existence, more than ho-hum, hum-drum, or so-so. In an earlier sermon I suggested there are times when fighting for survival, just hanging on, is about all we can muster. But surely life is intended for more than that! Surely life is not intended to be a sadistic struggle, proving only courage and endurance!

We also have explored what can and should follow times of survival: times of "getting it together." These are times marked by discipline, reflection, soul searching, and commitment. Hopefully, the fruits of this stage will be a clear direction in life, proper values and priorities, and a new faith in God's presence and power that has emerged out of our struggles.

The third phase in the "Beyond Survival" series is not intended to be temporary like the first two but rather a constant way of living, a final stage of the Christian life. I call this stage "letting go!" The other two stages work well with our natural instincts. That is, it is natural to want to survive, natural to try to "get it all together," to sort things out. But "letting go" is not so natural, not so easy.

"Letting go" is a new level of trusting, a new level of faith in God. It is more than surviving; it is thriving. It is more than struggling; it obtains the prizes of peace and joy. Maybe an analogy might help to distinguish between these three stages of: "hanging on," "getting it all together," and "letting go."

If you ever have fallen into deep water, you may understand what it means to struggle for survival—to frantically fight for air, to hang on tightly to the edge of a boat, to grab for anything to help you stay afloat. You simply hang on to survive. You don't worry about form, about your appearance, about what time it is. Your main objective is survival.

Several years ago I did what few novices should attempt to do—to fish alone from an eighteen-foot canoe! One person in a canoe is not the most stable arrangement—I can assure you! As I made a perfect cast to land a five-pound bass, the inevitable happened. I quickly was initiated into the Southern Baptist tradition. That's right—total immersion! (I would have preferred the Methodist tradition of sprinkling.) I suppose I never really was in danger. My life jacket quickly brought me back to the surface, but the cold lake water certainly got my attention, and I was careful to hang on tightly to my partially submerged canoe.

I was ready then for the second phase. I already had "hung on." Now I needed to "get it all together." I called for help and soon two friends came to my rescue in another canoe—one not filled with water.

It was now time for the third stage—"letting go." It was no longer necessary to fight to survive. I did not have to "keep it together." I was not even charting my course or trying to control things. I simply was trusting my friends to deliver me, to get me safely to solid ground.

When my friends arrived, they pulled me from the cold water, stretched me out in the center of the canoe, and paddled me to safety. Because I was no longer threatened, and had others who cared surrounding me, I could simply "let go." My experience at the lake took me through all the three stages.

> *Letting go is more like floating than swimming.*

Letting go is more like floating then swimming. In one sense it helps us survive the long haul because it saves our energy. Wouldn't it be nice to live for a while in the "letting go" realm where everything did not depend on us, where everything wasn't either a hassle or a struggle? Wouldn't it be nice to float for a while instead of fighting the water in panic or swimming without rest?

I'm not talking about a stage or phase without work, without pain, or without any discipline. But I am talking about a stage where we trust God more than we trust ourselves, where we see things from a broader perspective, where some of the things we once worried about no longer are our serious concern.

I'm talking about a way of life that is strongly connected to other people, where their problems and their pain are a part of our own. I'm talking about "letting go" of some of our concerns in order to grab hold of someone else's load. And as we do so, Jesus tells us that our "yoke is easy, and (our) burden . . . light" (Matt. 11:30).

Jesus, by his life and by his words, showed us that life is intended to be lived and celebrated and enjoyed. Our text contains one of the greatest promises and hopes of the Christian life. Jesus said, "I came that [you] may have life, and have it abundantly" (John 10:10*b*).

Jesus wants more for us than survival. He wants more than for people to just "have it together." He wants people to discover abundant living.

Have we experienced abundant living? Will we get stuck in phase one or phase two? Will we go through life as though it were only to be endured? Will we live as if we needed only self-discipline and hard work? Or will we go through life really living it, tasting it, feeling it, celebrating it, and loving it? Have you had any abundance lately? No, I'm not talking about material abundance. I mean, have you enjoyed life lately?

> *Jesus wants more for us than survival.*

Most of us are convinced in today's world that abundant living has been canceled due to stress. We seem to be convinced that our lives are destined to be stressed out. It is very easy to experience stress in our present-day culture. But part of our stress is our preoccupation with stress. We not only spend each day in stress but also spend each day thinking about spending each day in stress! Phase three of "letting go" cannot evolve, the abundant life is not ours, if we remain stressed, depressed, "regressed," or obsessed.

But there may be room for our being "possessed," if, that is, we understand that we are possessed by God. If we understand that God claims us, loves us, cares for us, then maybe we can begin to "let go," to trust more in God than in our own brilliance, to believe more in God than in the talents God gave us, to rely more on the Creator than on this small creature who will but live and die.

Letting go is not easy. It is far easier to rely on ourselves than to trust in God for our future and our well-being. It is so easy just to stay in stage two—it is so comfortable: we like to think we are in control.

Does anyone else besides me like stage two? Don't you like getting it together and trying to keep it together? Don't you like to regain control after losing it and to get those reigns back in your hands? Isn't it a confidence builder to think that we have finally gotten it together and that we will be able to plan out the rest of our lives and control the important things that will happen?

The problem is, phase two works only for a while. After phase two—getting it together, one either goes back to the survival stage or moves on to the final and ultimate stage of the Christian journey, the stage marked by letting go—letting go to God—trusting more in God than in ourselves.

Not all church members make it to stage three. Most, in fact, do not. Some of us never make it beyond survival—our frown lines and worry lines are deep enough to handle the runoff of a two-inch rain.

Some of us never make it out of phase two. You can spot us easily. We have callouses and blisters from holding the reins so tightly. We have spurs on our boots to keep things moving. We wear blinders because we want no distractions from our reaching our goals. Yes, there are people riding with us in the stagecoach but they do not control where we are headed. They are along just for the ride.

Some of us just get it all together and then think we can hold it together by ourselves—or with a little help in the emergencies. Little do we realize that we may be riding in the opposite direction of abundant living and inner peace. Little do we understand that if we do not learn to float, to relax in the love and power of God, we will not have the endurance to make it—the waves are too high, the journey too long.

May I recommend stage three to us all? I'm not there yet, though I believe a few of you are. I have just one foot under the rainbow. I'm trying to relax in God's love. I'm trying to let go. I'm trying to learn the secret of keeping my self-discipline without trying to carry all the weight. I'm trying to learn to float more often.

I suppose one answer to letting go is resting more in the love of God, to feel more deeply that we are loved and forgiven people. Isn't there a buoyancy when we know we are loved? Doesn't that put things in perspective? Doesn't that float us to the top?

Paul once thought he had it all together. He followed the law; he kept things in control, or thought he did. But later he discovered a freedom in God's love and power. Later he was able to rest in the thought that nothing could separate him from the love of God—nothing! His self-confidence became God-confidence. Then, instead of saying, "I'm the greatest," he could say, "I can do all things through [Christ] who strengthens me (Phil. 4:13)."

John Wesley, the founder of Methodism, knew the three stages I'm talking about. He barely survived his missionary experience in Georgia. He knew what it meant to "hang on." He spent much of his life "getting it together." Wesley not only got it together; he also organized it into neat little compartments. He was disciplined and efficient, committed and diligent.

But only when he "let go" did he discover peace of mind. Only when he finally accepted that God's love for him was bigger than anything else—only then could Wesley find life abundant. Wesley wrote, "I felt I did trust in Christ, Christ alone for my salvation; and an assurance was given me, that He had taken away my sins, even mine, and saved me from the law of sin and death." [12]

How do we get to phase three? If I were an expert I would already be there, but at least I am moving forward inch by inch under the vibrant colors of the rainbow. I think I am beginning, just beginning, to relax in God's love. Perhaps our first step is to understand that we are not yet there. If we just have it together, if the reins are tightly in our hands, then we are not there yet. We even may be headed in the wrong direction.

But there are some steps we can take. We can pray more. We can gain new priorities. We can accept God's assurance of being forgiven. We can stop swimming for a while and try to trust enough to float. We can give up the false and foolish idea that we ever could be in control of life.

All these things may help us move under the rainbow of God's love and find a new peace of mind. But we never should forget that we are not to make the journey alone—indeed we cannot. Unless we journey together we will not make it to our destination.

Remember one of the most important parts of "getting it together"? Jesus gave us a direction not only for that phase but also for every phase. To state it simply: "Love God and love your neighbor."

The real difference between abundant life and the "we got it together" life is this: In abundant life we are not only loving God and loving our neighbor but also finally experiencing for ourselves the love of God and neighbor.

In abundant life we are not only loving God and loving our neighbor but also finally experiencing for ourselves the love of God and neighbor.

It is the feeling, the assurance, of being loved that keeps us afloat, that allows us to have fun, that relaxes us and gives us new peace.

I don't know about you, but I am ready to move beyond survival. I am even ready to move beyond the "getting it together" stage. I am ready to float a little in life. I am ready to receive the gift of Christ's promise.

There's a time for "hanging on." There's a time for "getting it together," but the best time of all is when we finally can "let go" and let God!

When the LORD restored the fortunes of Zion, we were like those who dream. Then our mouth was filled with laughter, and our tongue with shouts of joy; then it was said among the nations, "The LORD has done great things for them." The LORD has done great things for us, and we rejoiced. Restore our fortunes, O LORD, like the watercourses in the Negeb. May those who sow in tears reap with shouts of joy. Those who go out weeping, bearing the seed for sowing, shall come home with shouts of joy, carrying their sheaves. Psalm 126

"A voice was heard in Ramah, wailing and loud lamentation, Rachel weeping for her children; she refused to be consoled, because they are no more." Matthew 2:18

Christmas at Ramah!

*H*ave you ever spent Christmas at Ramah? Have you ever heard mothers crying over the loss of their children? Have you ever had trouble receiving the good news of Jesus' birth because you were lonely, depressed, or grieving?

Christmas comes every year to Ramah. It comes to all cities and villages. It comes to anyone who will welcome the news of the Christ Child, and to those who receive its message there comes a deep joy, a joy even through tears!

In the Gospel of Matthew we are told the story of King Herod commanding the killing in Bethlehem of all male children two years and younger. Matthew follows the story with these words from Jeremiah:

> "A voice was heard in Ramah, wailing and loud lamentation, Rachel weeping for her children; she refused to be consoled, because they were no more." (Matt. 2:18)

Rachel, as you may recall, was the mother of Joseph and Benjamin and thus the ancestress of the children of Israel. In the book of Jeremiah, Rachel was weeping for her children in exile. But here her spirit weeps for the babies killed by Herod's men and for the families who lost them. Ramah is not far from Bethlehem where the soldiers performed their terrible deed.[13] Surely weeping and wailing could be heard throughout the countryside.

As I reflected upon this text, I detected a double tragedy. First, there was the tragedy of the slaughter of infants, infants who meant no harm, infants innocent of adult scheming and wickedness. What indeed could be more tragic than the loss of these little ones?

But this initial tragedy does not compare to the tragedy that follows, which is that the grief never ends. These mothers are never consoled. There will be no light to cast out the darkness. Despair will defeat hope! What word can we bring to these grieving mothers of Bethlehem? It was Jesus' birth that led to the death of their sons. Will the Christmas story remain a nightmare to them? Will it offer no hope? Will they never see that Jesus came bringing life, not death; that he gives hope, not despair; that he wipes away tears and shares with us a deep and abiding joy?

Can the angels' song be heard from Bethlehem to Ramah? Will the echo of "Gloria" hush their crying? Must one tragedy be followed by another? Will those who grieve refuse to be consoled? It is tragic to lose a child, but must they lose the Christ Child also? It is tragic to lose a spouse, but must one also forfeit the joy of Christmas? It is tragic to observe human suffering, but must that suffering rob us of hope?

> *It is tragic to observe human suffering, but must that suffering rob us of hope?*

The Christ Child comes to Ramah and to Bethlehem. This holy child will suffer no harm for now, but he will later know much suffering. He will later experience human sorrow. But this child was born to bring joyous life: abundant life and life eternal. No tragedy can destroy that good news!

Yet today Ramah is with us. Innocent children still die in Bethlehem, and India, and across our land. Good people still get sick. Saints of the church still die. There is still crying around us as we again prepare to sing "Joy to the World."

As Christians we may not always have a "Holly Jolly Christmas," for much may sadden us. But we can still have a joyous Christmas, a hopeful Christmas, one that is not afraid to embrace sadness with loving compassion, one that has learned to smile in the midst of tears, one that worships the Savior who can defeat tragedy.

> *Christians are ones who can speak of joy when all is not joyful.*

Christians are ones who can speak of joy when all is not joyful. They can announce the "light of the world" when there is still much darkness. They can offer love and hope to the mothers and fathers of Bethlehem and Ramah and even of our city. Yes, tragedy is forever with us. The innocent suffer. But as Christians we are ready and willing to be consoled. We do not desire to stay in our tombs or to feed on the darkness. In the midst of our darkness we may see clearly the Natal Star!

This year Christmas comes to many with heavy hearts. Some have lost loved ones. Some fear they may soon lose the ones they love. Some have concerns and anxieties over loved ones. Some are ill; and some are lonely.

If we have heavy hearts, "Jingle Bells" will probably not console us. But can we remain hopeless amid candlelight and the words and melody of "Silent Night"? Can we remain joyless as the faithful of our church sing "Joy to the World"? The theme of this sermon was reflected in an Advent devotion. Margaret Huffman writes:

> Is this the year when the joys of Christmas sound only as empty echoes in a once-happy marriage, split by divorce or death?
>
> Sadnesses are magnified at this time of year, when everything seems larger than life—even emptiness.
>
> It was such a year for the young woman who had suffered just about all there was to endure: illness, the death of her remaining parent, the end of a relationship. There was no way she could even imagine celebrating Christmas—until early in December, she received a brightly wrapped package from a friend. Inside was a tiny gold Christmas-tree lapel pin, with a note: "Wishing you even a little Christmas."
>
> "And that was all the Christmas I could celebrate that year," she explained, pointing to the minute gold pin on her lapel, where it has rested each holiday since that darkest one.
>
> "Some years, once again, it is about all I can muster, but a 'little Christmas' is always enough," she added.

Yet isn't just a fragment of hope better than none? Isn't a tiny celebration better than a dark, empty room? For isn't it sufficient to have faith as a mustard seed? For from such small seeds of faith can grow Christmas truths of all sizes, nourished sometimes by our own tears of pain.

No matter what pain might be preventing you from celebrating this year, imagine a tiny gold Christmas tree, pinned right there on your lapel. Then look in the mirror and wish yourself, "Merry Christmas, anyway."[14]

This year the Christ Child promises to come to Ramah and Bethlehem. The Christ Child will come where angels sing and where mothers cry. The Christ who comes promises to bring us joy, a joy not filled with frivolous laughter but with a laughter that comes even in the midst of tears and in spite of grief or discouragement.

Tragedy will not come to everyone's door this year. Some of us have received good news. Some are recovering from illness. Some have had a close call with death and are now doing much better. Some of us have new jobs or a new hope of keeping old ones. Some of us have witnessed positive transformations in people we love and have a new hope for their future.

But all of us know those who live in Ramah this year. We all know of those who are hurting. So we may have compassion for them and reach out to them. But we need not be in total despair for them, for even in their situation there is hope. So perhaps we simply wish for them the brightest Christmas they can have. We say to them in our hearts, "Have a Merry Christmas, anyway!" And we are somehow consoled—as hopefully they are consoled—by the news of a Christ Child coming into our world and into our lives.

If you have ever experienced in your family the birth of a child or grandchild following the death of a family member you know that such a new life brings a very special kind of joy. It is a joy that does not stop the tears, but it does wipe them away.

The gift of the Christ Child is such a gift. The Christ Child does not eliminate all tragedy, but he makes all tragedy infinitely more bearable, and he adds to our experience the welling up of a very deep joy.

Melvin Wheatley, in his marvelous book *Christmas Is for Celebrating*, teaches us that there is much to celebrate each and every Christmas:

> Not a world that has in it nothing but good, but
> a world that is good, while having in it so
> much that is bad;
> Not a life that knows no darkness, but a life in
> which even those who walk in darkness have
> seen a great light;
> Not a God who gives us everything we want, but
> a God who gives us everything we have, and
> offers us all we need, now and forever. [15]

This year there will be crying in Ramah, Bosnia, South Africa, and the United States. And some of those crying will refuse to be consoled. Some will choose to double their tragedy because this Christmas they will not listen for the angels' song. They will not look for the light that shines in the darkness!

But to all who turn their ear toward Bethlehem's song, to all who follow a star in the midst of shadows, to all who listen for the word of good news, there will be a comfort and even more—there will be a deep, deep joy!

The wise men knew, the shepherds knew, the angels knew what we now know—that there is nothing that can happen to us that prevents the possibility of God consoling us.

Whether you live in Ramah or Bethlehem or in this city, crying can be heard. This Christmas the Christ Child comes to all of us—and when he comes he will never, never leave us.

Paul's Christmas card to us is quite unique. On the outside we see the image of Christ. On the inside we read these words:

> What then are we to say about these things? If God is for us, who is against us? . . . Who will separate us from the love of Christ? Will hardship, or distress, or persecution, or famine, or nakedness, or peril, or sword? . . . No, in all these things we are more than conquerors through him who loved us. For I am convinced that neither death, nor life, nor angels, nor rulers, nor things present, nor things to come, nor powers, nor height, nor depth, nor anything else in all creation, will be able to separate us from the love of God in Christ Jesus our Lord.   (Rom. 8:31, 35, 37-39)

There is still crying in Bethlehem and Ramah. Good people become ill. The saints still die. But the Christ Child still comes. The light still shines. And the darkness will never, never, never overcome it!

Notes

1. Jean Van Dyke, ed., *Words to Live By* (Fort Atkinson, Wis., *Farming Magazine;* Greendale, Wis., *Country Magazine,* 1990), p. 34.

2. Ibid.

3. William Cowper, "God Moves in a Mysterious Way," *The Book of Hymns* (Nashville: The United Methodist Publishing House, 1964, 1966), no. 215.

4. *Interpretation* (Atlanta: John Knox Press, 1987), p. 118.

5. Victor Paul Furnish, *2 Corinthians* (Garden City, NY: Doubleday & Company, Inc., 1984), p. 549.

6. *Interpretation* (Atlanta: John Knox Press, 1987), p. 118.

7. William Barclay, *The Daily Study Bible Series, The Letters to the Corinthians* (Philadelphia: The Westminster Press, 1954, 1956), p. 41.

8. *The Daily Study Bible Series, Romans,* William Barclay, 184.

9. Ernest Best, *The Cambridge Bible Commentary, the Letter of Paul to Romans* (Cambridge: University of Cambridge Press), p. 146.

10. Richard Selzer, *Mortal Lessons* (Touchstone Books: New York, N.Y., 1987) pp. 45-46.

11. Zan Holmes, Sermon given at the Academy for Preaching, Nashville, Tenn., 1989.

12. Albert C. Outler, ed., *John Wesley* (New York: Oxford University Press, 1964), p. 66.

13. Eduard Schweizer, *The Good News According to Matthew,* trans. David Green (Atlanta: John Knox Press, 1975), p. 44.

14. Margaret Anne Huffman, *Advent, A Calendar of Devotions* (Nashville: Abingdon Press, 1992,), pp. 20-21.

15. Melvin Wheatley, *Christmas Is for Celebrating* (Nashville: The Upper Room, 1977), p. 22.